RESPONSIBLE JOURNALISM

SOME OTHER VOLUMES IN THE
SAGE FOCUS EDITIONS

RESPONSIBLE JOURNALISM

Edited by
Deni Elliott

SAGE PUBLICATIONS
The Publishers of Professional Social Science
Beverly Hills   Newbury Park   London   New Delhi

For information address:

SAGE Publications, Inc.
275 South Beverly Drive
Beverly Hills, California 90212

SAGE Publications Inc.
2111 West Hillcrest Drive
Newbury Park
California 91320

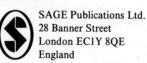

SAGE Publications Ltd.
28 Banner Street
London EC1Y 8QE
England

SAGE PUBLICATIONS India Pvt. Ltd.
M-32 Market
Greater Kailash I
New Delhi 110 048 India

Printed in the United States of America

Library of Congress Cataloging-in-Publication Data

Main entry under title:

Responsible journalism.

   (Sage focus editions ; 83)
   Includes index.
   1. Journalistic ethics—Addresses, essays, lectures.
I. Elliott, Deni.
PN4756.R48   1986   174'.9097   86-1759
ISBN 0-8039-2611-1
ISBN 0-8039-2612-X (pbk.)

FIRST PRINTING

CONTENTS

INTRODUCTION

In the three years I've been doing ethics seminars with editors and reporters, I've been continually reminded about how much practitioners disagree when deciding how journalists ought to act in specific situations. I've also been continually struck by the amount of agreement concerning underlying assumptions of the business. Practitioners disagree about whether a particular item should have been published, about whether intrusion on a story subject's personal life was warranted or not. Yet they have (sometimes unspoken) agreement on some basic issues: Journalists should make these determinations, not some outside agency; the "newsworthiness" of an item dictates its treatment; and, even though journalists may ultimately choose to publish an item that will cause harm to an individual or that will disturb some readers or listeners, there is agreement that the conscientious journalist does so knowingly, and only after due consideration of the effect that the publication will have.

I am not naively suggesting that these agreements are always based on "ethical" grounds. But whether the grounds are economic, conventional, or philosophical, the bottom-line assumption is the same: When operating in the role of information gatherer or information provider, journalists do have some responsibility to some individuals or groups. However, it is clear that those responsibilities may be met in different ways through the many situations that come up in the newsroom.

The authors included in this book have taken on the difficult task of trying to pin down just where journalistic responsibilities come from, how responsibilities fit in with legal and press theories, and how they play out in specific contexts.

In some respects, this book is reflective of the discussions that practitioners have. Along with the competing perspectives presented here, there are also some fundamental areas of agreement.

Yet these essays do more than simply illustrate the debate that continues in U.S. newsrooms and classrooms. The authors have looked behind the judgments of whether specific actions are responsible or not. Each offers a sophisticated line of argument, identifying philosophical, legal, or contextual bases for accepting particular conclusions about journalistic responsibility. In doing so, criteria for making judgments are clarified.

The first section of the book addresses the basic foundations of journalistic responsibility.

In Chapter 1, Hodges considers what it means to say that any person has responsibility, and works from there toward a definition of press responsibility. He argues that journalists take on responsibilities through "covenants" with society and through obligations that are "self-imposed." He identifies four functions—political, educational, utility, and cultural—that news media take responsibility for performing in society.

I provide a philosophical base for news media responsibilities in Chapter 2, arguing that specific obligations can be derived through the power held by the institutional media and through the promises that news organizations implicitly or explicitly make to the communities they serve.

The second section of the book concerns two relationships: between news media responsibilities and legal theory and between news media responsibilities and press theory.

In Chapter 3, Merrill argues that the only acceptable U.S. theory of press responsibility is "that which is pluralistically defined or determined by the individual journalists themselves." According to Merrill, legally determined responsibilities, or those accepted institutionally, contradict the libertarian ideals that form the foundation for U.S. press theory.

Barney does further work with the notion of pluralism in Chapter 4. But he focuses on the need for pluralism in informational content. Journalists, in Barney's view, must be committed to providing the wide range of information and perspectives that are necessary for a participatory democracy.

Glasser, too, is concerned about suppression of information needed for a participatory democracy. In Chapter 5, he argues for an "affirmative" reading of the First Amendment through which "freedom and responsibility stand side by side—distinct and yet inseparable." The state, according to Glasser, should act to protect citizens from nongovernmental as well as governmental suppression of expression.

In Chapter 6, Dennis addresses another aspect of First Amendment freedom and implied responsibility—that of news media as representative of the people. He raises the question, "Is the press really the representative of the people or is it a usurper, a self-appointed representative pushing its own point of view rather than that of its constituents?"

Christians completes this section with an argument that news media do, indeed, have a responsibility that relates to representation theory, that of presenting a "representative picture" of society. In Chapter 7, he provides a theoretical base for an advocacy role of the press. According to Christians, "the litmus test of whether or not the news profession fulfills its mission over the long term is its advocacy for those outside the socioeconomic establishment."

The last section of the book considers how press responsibility plays out in two specific contexts.

In Chapter 8, Linsky discusses the participatory function news media have in federal policymaking. He argues that no longer can journalists act as though they "simply report the news"; no longer can they act as though their relationship with government is "adversarial." The power that the press has in policymaking implies responsibilities other than those that follow from a traditional reading of media function.

Ziff completes the discussion of responsibility with a careful examination of the universal principles that are assumed to guide the daily conduct of all U.S. news media. In Chapter 9, he presents an alternative to the "cosmopolitan" or anonymous-metropolitan model upon which most current journalistic obligations are based. He argues that an alternative "provincial" model, which has at its core "the maintenance, correction, and adornment of the local community," can be offered as an equally viable structure for journalistic practice.

The competing perspectives presented within this book raise some of the basic questions of the press responsibility debate:

(1) Is the proper role for journalists that of advocate or neutral observer, or is it whatever journalists decide for themselves in each situation? Once a stand is taken on that assumption, how can we expect journalists to act in fulfilling that role?

(2) Where ought journalistic loyalties lie? What, if anything, do journalists owe to their community? What do they owe to the craft? What do they owe to themselves?

(3) Who should determine journalistic responsibilities? Should they be decided through the historical purpose for our current press freedoms? Through broader social and political theory or through ethical theory? Should they be decided by the consumers of news? By government? By institutional journalism or by individual practitioners?

Even though the authors would answer these questions in very different ways (and some might even reject some of the questions as invalid), we do share some essential assumptions.

First, we assume that journalism is not, and should not be, primarily a self-serving endeavor. Obligation is implicit in the journalistic role, whether it is seen as obligation to society or obligation to preserve a multiplicity of views on the journalistic role.

There is a related assumption that responsible journalism is journalism with a conscience. We operate on the assumption that journalists should be self-aware, that they should think about their role, and should think about the consequences of their views as well.

Perhaps most important, we share an assumption that there is a need for journalists and academics to work at developing criteria by which to judge responsible journalism. We share no hope, of course, that singularly or collectively, we've "gotten it right, once and for all." The ideas and ideals of journalistic responsibility set up a dynamic conversation within newsrooms, within classrooms, and between news media and their audiences. To "get it right, once and for all" would deny the changes brought about through technological advance, economic imperatives, demographic swings, and all of the other variable factors that make society itself continually evolving.

As society continues to evolve, specific obligations for news media evolve as well. Now, as always, there is a need for that relationship between media and society to be addressed in a new way, in a way that addresses current societal function as well as institutional freedoms.

—Deni Elliott
Utah State University
August 1986

PART I

Foundations

If you ask people why journalists should act responsibly, they'll often cite the First Amendment to the U.S. Constitution. Yet that answer is wrong and would be frightening if it were true.

The First Amendment guarantees freedom with no cautionary statement as to how freedom of speech or the press should be exercised. The Constitution protects seemingly irresponsible speech along with the responsible. In fact, the democracy the First Amendment protects depends on people being allowed to make statements that others might view as irresponsible. When college students first spoke out publicly against the Vietnam War, for example, many thought that the students were being irresponsible in not supporting the U.S. war effort. Listening to and thinking about "irresponsible" statements and opinions that are different from our own create major changes in a democratic society.

While the authors of these chapters would not all agree that responsibility is in the eye of the beholder, they would agree that it is sometimes difficult to decide if action is objectively responsible or not.

Let's assume for a minute that the concept of responsibility could be completely defined. And, let's strengthen the First Amendment by adding an additional assumption that guaranteed freedoms ethically imply duties to use those freedoms in responsible ways. The First Amendment would still not be adequate as the sole basis for responsible journalism. If it were true that the First Amendment provided the necessary condition for press responsibility, then we could logically conclude that without the First Amendment, journalists would not have to act in a responsible manner.

This reasoning structure can be shown in a different way. It's like saying that murder is only wrong because it is against the law. We have legal sanctions against murder, but surely there is a prior moral duty for people not to commit murder.

It would be a little frightening if journalists should act responsibly only because of the First Amendment. Obviously, it would mean that journalists in countries without First Amendment freedoms would have no reason to act in a responsible manner. It would place us in a position of ethical legalism where we implicitly claim that it is the law that makes actions right or wrong rather than the law merely putting on paper what is already known to be right or wrong.

We start this survey at the very beginning, looking for a strong philosophical base for journalistic responsibility. How can we tell if journalists are acting responsibly? Why should they act responsibly? These questions cannot be answered for specific situations without theories about the nature of responsibility. The First Amendment itself is a principle based on underlying theory.

In Chapters 1 and 2, theories of responsibility are constructed through consideration of the following questions:

(1) How do people come to have responsibilities at all?
(2) What responsibilities follow from the function mass media have in society?
(3) How does the power of the media entail responsibilities?
(4) What explicit and implicit promises have the media made to their audiences?
(5) What responsibility do individual journalists have when they are employed by the institutional news media?

1

DEFINING PRESS RESPONSIBILITY: A FUNCTIONAL APPROACH

Louis W. Hodges

Everyone knows what responsibility doctors have. Society assigns them the function of seeing to the health of the nation. Everyone knows the responsibility of lawyers. Theirs is to oversee the system of justice. Or, in the language of the American Bar Association (1980), lawyers function "as guardians of the law." Similarly, everyone knows the responsibilities of educators, the clergy, accountants, and politicians. But what about journalists? What functions may society legitimately expect journalists to perform? What should we turn over to them? What ought the serious journalist accept responsibility for doing? In short, what can and should be the role and function of the press in our liberal democracy?

These questions go to the heart of the ethics of journalism. They invite thoughtful journalists (and the readers / viewers they serve) to ask, "Exactly what is it that I am about?" "If I perform well, what contribution can I make to the building of a better society?" "What is it that I am willing for others to expect of me?" "For what will I accept responsibility?"

Unless these questions are answered satisfactorily, neither journalists nor the public they serve can give an adequate moral evaluation of the performance of the press. Nor can the journalist, absent some understanding of these responsibilities, obtain much guidance in daily decisions (e.g., "Is that particular invasion of privacy justifiable or not?").

For purposes of this essay, we need to distinguish at the outset between *responsibility* and *accountability*. Although modern dictionaries do not always define these words differently, they can, and should, have different meanings. The issue of "responsibility" is the following: To what social needs should we expect journalists to respond ably? The issue of "accountability" is as follows: How might society call on journalists to account for their performance of the responsibilities given them? Responsibility has to do with defining proper conduct; accountability with compelling it. The former concerns identification; the latter concerns power. The issue of responsibility is a practical one the answer to which can come from an examination of the society's needs to know and the press's abilities to inform. The issue of accountability is a political one the answer to which can come from an analysis of centers of power—government, media organizations, public influence.

The distinction is clearly reflected in the common language. Notice the prepositions: We talk about being "responsible *for*" but "account-able *to.*" For example, we may be responsible for the accuracy of the information we deliver, for informing the reader about government, for not invading privacy or inflicting further hurt on victims of tragedy. But we are accountable to a government, an editor, a court, a boss.

This distinction can be made by using other terms. To talk about responsibility is to talk about the content of our moral duties and obligations, about the substance of what we should do. To talk about accountability is to talk about who can or should have power to demand, through persuasion or threat, that we discharge those duties well. Questions of responsibility focus on the nature and function of the press, on the criteria rational people might use to access press performance. Questions of accountability focus on the freedom of the press, on how someone might command the press to follow those criteria.

It is possible to have a press that is both free and responsible. Such a press would simply be one that voluntarily (read "freely") understood the proper role of the press and played it well. It is not possible, however, to have a press that is both totally free and accountable. Such a press could not be free to choose voluntarily to behave responsibly because any authority who could "call the press to give account of itself" could require responsible performance.

The question of responsibility is logically prior to the question of accountability. We can decide what we think the press should be responsible for without looking for ways to compel press performance. We cannot, however, reasonably seek to coerce responsible press performance until we have first defined responsible performance. We cannot reasonably demand that the press give an account of itself or improve its performance until we determine what it is the press is responsible for doing.

The distinction between responsibility and accountability is important for several reasons. There has been little serious inquiry by practicing journalists in this country into press responsibility. Part of the reason for that is our failure to separate the issues adequately. When the question of press responsibility comes up among journalists, they frequently jump immediately to the issue of accountability and become defensive, properly protective of First Amendment prerogatives. Here is a conversation that illustrates the point.

Lou: This story seems to me to invade the rape victim's privacy unduly. Do you think you need to do that?

Editor: The public has a right to know about rapes in this community.

Lou: Yes, but maybe not the details of this particular rape. Do you think you should establish a policy of not reporting the victims' names? Would that not be the responsible thing to do?

Editor: I don't want to be responsible to anyone. If we are going to have a free press then no one ought to be able to tell me what to do. It is the editor's prerogative.

It is clear that I was talking about what the policy ought to be; the editor was concerned about who should make policy. Both are legitimate questions, but until we distinguish them we will not get far in sober reflection on the several functions (responsibilities) of the press. The mind that feels threatened by loss of authority is not entirely free to be inquisitive, analytical, and reflective.

Journalists' sensitivity to the political issue of accountability is more to be applauded than condemned. Democracy demands a fiercely independent press, especially one free from accountability to government. The power of the press and questions of power over the press are legitimate concerns, but we dare not let that fact stifle serious efforts to define press responsibility. Although there is good reason for the press to be wary, defensive, and resistant about matters of accountability, there is no reason for the same wariness about responsibility. That inquiry can and should be made in dispassionate ways free from the intellectually paralyzing emotions that accountability stirs in the human breast.

The purpose of this essay, then, is to work toward a definition of press responsibility. I want to lay aside issues of accountability. Before we can successfully address the question of press responsibility, however, we must inquire into the very nature of responsibility itself. We need to ask just how it is that human beings come to have responsibilities to each other.

THE GROUND OF RESPONSIBILITY

It is a fact of life that human beings are inescapably and simultaneously both individual and social. We are free agents living together, whose actions affect each other, and who are radically dependent upon each other. Those facts dictate that we must be responsible to and for each other. Individual responsibility is meaningful only in light of social existence. There is a long history of complex debate over the basis of moral responsibility, but the above claims seem indisputable. We agree that we have responsibilities to each other.

At some level of generality there is even wide agreement on what those responsibilities are, at least in a *prima facie* sense. We agree to the minimal principle, for instance, that we owe it to others not to harm them. We agree that we owe it to each other to seek together to meet each other's needs. Most of us would agree at much more concrete levels: for example, that we have a duty not to drive an automobile while drunk, not to throw paint on a neighbor's door, and not to give poisoned candy to children.

So the roots of responsibility per se lie in the fact that we are both individual and social beings whose decisions and actions inevitably affect others. The very fact that we have the ability or power to affect each other deeply, either for good or for ill, requires that we act responsibly toward each other if society is to endure.

The greater our power or ability to affect others becomes, the heavier becomes our moral duty. That is the general practical ground of the notion of responsibility.

At a more concrete level, however, we must ask how it is that a person or group comes to have obligations to or for other persons or groups. Within what kind of relationships do we take on specific responsibilities to others? I think there are at least three.

ASSIGNED

In some human relationships, obligations and responsibilities are simply assigned by party A to party B. In an employer-employee relationship, for example, the employer determines the responsibility of an employee. In an authoritarian state, the sovereign simply assigns duties to those under sovereign authority. Responsibility and obligation dictated in this manner are possible, of course, only in those relations in which a significant power imbalance prevails. Once the relationship is established, party A is in a position simply to demand responsible conduct from B—and on A's terms. Military hierarchy is the clearest example of responsibility assigned by a superior to an inferior. The teacher-student relationship is another.

CONTRACTED

Some relationships, however, are between parties who share more equally in power and authority. Both A and B choose to exchange obligations and responsibilities. They enter a mutually binding contract. Sometimes, the contract is formal with the responsibilities of each party consciously agreed to. Formal contracts normally require a written document. The parties to the contract are essentially equal in power, at least in the sense that either is free to enter or not enter it. Once the formal contract has been entered, the obligations of party to party are firm and clearly understood by both.

Some contracts, on the other hand, are informal. No specific obligations may be stated, and certainly not all of them are. Obligations are implicit. The marriage relationship is an example of such an informal and uncodified contract. The marriage vows ordinarily state little more than that two persons have consented together in wedlock and that they will henceforth be regarded as husband and wife. The informal character of the vows does not entail that no specific obligations exist nor that the responsibilities are any less binding. Certain responsibilities and obligations are perceived by both parties to exist in consequence of a relationship consciously and deliberately entered. The moral duty of each party to be responsible is inherent in the voluntary character of the contract. To choose to enter a contract and to receive its benefits, whether formal or informal, is ipso facto to accept the moral duty to recognize and discharge the responsibilities it entails.

In both assigned and contracted responsibility, accountability is secured through more or less overt sanctions. If the student does not do what the teacher assigns and is consistently irresponsible in the discharge of duty, punishments are available to bring the wayward student into line and to encourage him or her to take obligations more seriously. In contracted obligation there is always a penalty in that if party A is irresponsible, that is, violates the terms of the contract, the contract is said to be "broken." Party B is thus relieved of responsibility and obligation to A.

SELF-IMPOSED

Sometimes in human affairs people will identify ways in which they might—but are not expected or required to—benefit another person or group and will in consequence voluntarily accept responsibility for doing so. The choice is an expression of character or virtue. Self-imposed responsibilities are no less real or binding as a result of the absence of compelling external authority or of an enforceable contract. Indeed, self-imposed responsibility may for a variety of human reasons be stronger and more enduring than assigned or contracted responsibility. For example, the "good Samaritan" role—played by one who finds a stranger in distress and who, without expectation of reward, seeks to relieve that distress—makes strong appeal to our individual sense of our own dignity and nobility. In the case of self-imposed responsibility, then, we choose to accept responsibilities as an expression of who we are.

In summarizing the three different sorts of responsibility, I should note only one more point. An individual's reason for acting responsibly differs according to the way responsibility is incurred. In the case of assigned responsibility, agents behave responsibly out of threat of power, or simply because they have no power to act otherwise, or out of respect for authority. When responsibility is contracted, the reason for responsible conduct lies in voluntarily accepted duty to others and in the general duty to keep promises. The reason for responding to self-imposed obligations is that one owes it to oneself to be a person of principle and character.

THE ROOTS OF PRESS RESPONSIBILITY

When we turn from the question of responsibility in general to the issue of responsibilities of the press, we can usefully employ these three classes of obligations. All three kinds of obligation exist for the press.

ASSIGNED RESPONSIBILITIES

In some societies, the responsibilities of the press are assigned by the government, or so it appears to the outside observer. The press is simply another arm of government. That is the pattern in much of the world. But in the United States, the press has relatively few assigned responsibilities. The government imposes the negative duties not to be libelous, not to defame, not to invade privacy, and so on, but we don't assign positive duties, such as a "duty" to report the mayor's speech. The U.S. press is remarkably free to decide on its own course of action.

Individual journalists, on the other hand, are assigned all sorts of responsibilities within the news organizations that employ them. The reporter is assigned to cover specific beats or events. Editors are told through company policy what kinds of responsibilities, both negative and positive, they have. Most journalists work within a hierarchy of authority. Good journalists take the responsibilities established by that authority seriously.

CONTRACTED RESPONSIBILITIES

In the United States the press comes to have responsibilities chiefly through an implied covenant with the society. The covenant is not formally contracted and written, of course, but that fact does not render it less real. Society seems to promise the press freedom to function with the assumption that the press will serve society's needs for information and opinion. In terms of form, the covenant is closely analogous to marriage (except for the license). The specific obligations are not clearly defined. They must be worked out informally on a continuing basis between specific press organizations and their audiences. Organizations pay attention to what their audiences need and want. Audiences are free within limits to choose which organization's products they will read or watch.

Individual journalists, however, typically are engaged in two contracts, one with the news organization and one with the reader/viewer. Individual responsibilities to the organization tend to be more explicitly and formally defined than are responsibilities to the audience. Ideally, because both the news organization and the individual journalist are in covenant with the audience, the terms of the contract between organization and individual will reflect the purposes of service to the audience.

The professional journalist's covenant with those who read or hear him or her is central. But its terms have been left vague and undefined. Greater clarification and definition are needed if professional journalists are to discharge responsibility more fully. The burden of definition of responsibility must lie chiefly at the feet of the journalist, but responsibilities must finally be identified by giving attention to the needs of the audience.

SELF-IMPOSED RESPONSIBILITIES

The third way people come to have responsibilities to others is by self-imposition. Individual journalists can, and the best ones do, develop a sense of what they are all about. They can build in their own minds a sense of excellent performance. They can commit themselves to their highest standards by dint of will, for the sake of principle and in service to others. These people regard the decision to be a journalist as a good deal more than a decision to take a job in the newsroom. They see it as a "calling," a *vocatio* to use Martin Luther's term. It is as though they are summoned by forces outside themselves to become special and to take on special obligations.

It is true, of course, that not everybody in newsrooms has made a conscious and deliberate decision to be a journalist. Sometimes upon meeting a reporter for the first time I ask, "What do you do?" The answer is frequently that "I work for the *Gazette*." But others reply, "I am a journalist." There is a difference. It includes a difference in self-perception and a difference in the individual's sense of responsibility. The person who has decided to "be a journalist" acknowledges a primary responsibility to the audience. The person who "works for the *Gazette*" admits primary responsibility to the boss. The former is far more likely than the latter to impose obligations on him- or herself.

THE CONTENT OF JOURNALISTS' RESPONSIBILITY

Thus far I have discussed only the forms responsibility takes in journalism. We now must turn to its content.

The question of press responsibility can be approached at three levels. First, we can inquire into the possible *functions* or social roles appropriate to journalism. Second, we can ask what are the *principles* that must guide the press if it is to perform those functions well, that is, "responsibly." Third, we can look for the kinds of *actions* journalists should and should not take if they would be obedient to those principles. Indeed, these three levels of responsibility can be seen to encompass journalism ethics in its entirety. I shall address only the first in this essay.

 In my view the press should take responsibility for performing four functions. The first is a *political* function. By informing the citizenry of what its government and other centers of power are doing, the press becomes itself an integral part of the political process. By monitoring the centers of power—political, economic, and social—the press functions to keep them in check.

The second role of the press involves an *educational* function. It includes reporting on and promoting discussion of ideas, opinions, and truths toward the end of social refinement of those ideas, opinions, and truths. In this role the press follows the tradition of the town meeting.

Third, the press functions as a *utility*, a conduit of information about what is happening. It operates as the society's "bulletin board."

The fourth function is social or *cultural*. The press holds up a mirror to society and reflects the kind of people we are, shows us our heroes and villains, recalls our shared values. We must now examine each of these in more detail.

THE POLITICAL ROLE

Representative government cannot exist (and cannot even be theoretically conceived) unless provision is made for the governed to know what their governors are doing, are not doing, and are contemplating doing. Because not every citizen can have personal access to the halls of government—executive, legislative, and judicial—each citizen needs to have representative eyes watching government on his or her behalf. Journalists are those who watch for us and report to us about our governors. It is a matter of practical necessity! Because we cannot all be there all of the time with our own eyes, ears, and tongue, we require that someone else be there. We "send" journalists to watch government on our behalf. Journalists thus become a vital practical link in the chain of communications. (As business organizations come to wield greater and greater power, they too are proper objects of press scrutiny. We need to know how these centers of power are affecting our lives.)

The claim that we need the press to "watch" for us in order that representative government can work rests on certain assumptions. One is the belief that power tends to corrupt. Those who have power, given the apparent propensities of human beings toward self-aggrandizement, will, if left unconstrained, arrogate more power to themselves in an ever ascending spiral. They can be constrained only by an informed populace. And it is the "bad news" of the corruption of power by governments that the public needs most to hear. "Good news" about governments can be reassuring, but it is knowledge of bad news that places real power in the hands of the people and enables them to rule.

But when it functions well in this role of government watcher, the press itself becomes a powerful political force. The fact that those who govern know they are being watched places reins on their power. Thus the very existence of the press serves to reduce the likelihood of usurpation of power by those who govern. Governors who know that they are being watched have to take the people into account in ways they otherwise would not. Although the press cannot itself prevent the corruption of office, it can inform the people who have the power to do so. The people depend absolutely upon knowledge of government in order to participate in the political process. The press is not the only source of that knowledge, but in our large and complex world it is and will remain the primary source.

The press has power in two ways. First, it has the power (freedom) to decide what to report and how. It can determine the quality of its reportage. Readers and viewers have relatively little capacity to influence, much less to control, press performance. Second, the very existence of the press serves to give notice to centers of power (governmental, economic, and social) that they are being watched and will be held accountable by the people.

There is some dispute about just how much real power the press actually has. Hodding Carter III reminds us of the limits on the power of the press:

> It is a continuing surprise to me to hear . . . the notions of the great power that the press is supposed to be wielding independent of all other aspects of society.
>
> I know we all like to bask either in the glow of Watergate or worry about its consequences, but . . . it took one second rate judge and some leaked grand jury proceedings, not the work of two cub reporters, to bring the real consequences of that event about. (Modern Media Institute, 1983)

On the other hand we must remember that had there been no cub reporters to whom proceedings could be leaked, had there been no journalists to recognize and report to the people on those proceedings, those who governed might well have been successful in their cover-up. Thus, although the press has little direct power, as a practical matter its presence as an effective conduit between the governed and their governors remains essential.

THE EDUCATIONAL ROLE

If we are to be a free and self-governing people, we require a special kind of education. I do not have in mind education as formal and systematic learning in a discipline (e.g., history, chemistry, medicine), though that learning is essential to self-governance as well. Nor do I have in mind education conceived as the mere transfer of information to society at large. Those forms of learning can be accomplished through many agencies including schools, libraries, churches, and governments.

The special educational need the press is singularly equipped to meet involves refinement and testing of those political, religious, and moral ideas and ideals that we use in shaping our individual and corporate lives. For that we require a truly public forum. It is a form of education that occurs best when conflicting opinions can face each other in open debate. It occurs when each opinion is freely expressed, making its own appeal, revealing the weakness of contrary opinions. Its subjects are the ideas, opinions, truths, and principles on which we have to rely in the shaping of public policy. Public discussion is the only viable way of refining and disseminating our thoughts on such matters, and the refinement of thought on such matters is an absolute precondition for wise public policy in a democratic state.

Perhaps a look at John Stuart Mill (1951) will uncover not only the nature of the need but also the reasons why public debate is absolutely essential to liberal democracy. Mill offers four reasons why liberty of thought and discussion is essential. The first is that only through discussion can we rectify mistakes in judgment.

> It is owing to a quality of the human mind, . . . that his errors are corrigible. He is capable of rectifying his mistakes, by discussion and experience. Not by experience alone. There must be discussion to show how experience is to be interpreted. Wrong opinions and practices gradually yield to fact and argument; but facts and arguments, to produce any effect on the mind, must be brought before it. Very few facts are able to tell their own story, without comments to bring out their meaning. (p. 108)

No activity, in short, is as likely to unseat false opinion as an unfettered encounter with truer ones.

Second, even in the case of true opinions, vigorous discussion is required if opinions are to retain their vitality: "However true it [an opinion] may be, if it is not fully, frequently, and fearlessly discussed, it will be held as a dead dogma, not a living truth" (Mill, 1951, p. 126). History shows that opinions that are not discussed and forever challenged soon lose their capacity to inspire the mind and motivate to action. They become essentially useless and eventually disappear from the consciousness of a culture.

Third, discussion is essential to fill out the partial truth contained in most of our opinions.

> We have hitherto considered only two possibilities; that the received opinion may be false, and some other opinion, consequently, true; or that, the received opinion being true, a conflict with the opposite error is essential to a clear apprehension and deep feeling of its truth. But there is a commoner case than either of these; when the conflicting doctrines,

instead of being one true and the other false, share the truth between them; and the nonconforming opinion is needed to supply the remainder of the truth, of which the received doctrine embodies only a part. (Mill, 1951, p. 140)

Human understanding of complex social, moral, and political principles or ideals is always halting and incomplete. No individual can possess all the insight and wisdom necessary to build a just state. Even if one could, the partial understanding of others would have to be improved if they are to participate in a democratic state. Our best hope for deepening insight and refining understanding, Mill claims, is through open, public, and rigorous inquiry.

Fourth, deprived of public discussion of opinions we will lose not merely the feeling of their importance but also their very meaning. Ideas will become mere dogmas formally professed, "inefficacious for good, but cumbering the ground, and preventing the growth of any real and heartfelt conviction, from reason or personal experience" (Mill, 1951, p. 149).

We might add the observation that in a pluralistic society knit together in so many complex ways trying desperately to work out a common destiny, the need for public discussion of and inquiry into ideas and ideals is all the greater. What was required in Mill's nineteenth-century England is required today in the United States in spades.

The need for the public forum cannot be seriously doubted. But why should we look to the press to provide it and to stimulate the exchange? The reason is simple: No other institutions on the horizon can meet the need as effectively and effficiently.

We used to have the town meeting, the chautauqua, debating societies, and pamphleteers. Through them a smaller civilization exchanged ideas and opinions about the great issues of the day. Out of that exchange opinions and ideas emerged in more refined form. We gained a new sense of the importance and vitality of old ideas. We gained insight into new ideas. We stripped away layers of partial truths and did come closer to knowing the truth. But these forums no longer exist. It is a matter of fact that public debate takes place today chiefly in the pages of daily newspapers, television panels, and (to a lesser extent) in broadcast editorials and commentary.

Exchange takes place elsewhere as well. Certain classes in society exchange opinions through books, learned journals, and university forums. But these people tend to be elite specialists, the professionals. If only they carry on the debate, they will become the only class capable of forming public policy. We would then, in effect, have abandoned democracy for oligarchy.

Specialized publications such as the *National Review* enhance public debate, but I suspect that the effect on Buckley's special audience is not education but reinforcement of already-held partial truths. The same may be true for ecclesiastical publications such as the United States Methodist *Advocate*. Unfortunately, such publications are rarely as open as the secular press is to the important truth often found in unpopular opinion.

The educational function of the press is now performed in a variety of ways. Syndicated columnists play an important role, for example, when the columns of George Will, Ellen Goodman, and David Broder all appear on the same page of the *Washington Post*. Better results could be obtained, perhaps, if each journalist were to address the same subject on a given day. That is obviously not possible, and maybe not desirable. Yet we have seen the advent of a single-subject forum on the "Opinion" page of *USA Today*. There we have a single issue or subject explored by individuals with sometimes widely divergent opinions. Another plus for *USA Today* is the inclusion of opinions espoused by ordinary people as well as by professionals.

The press plays the educational role through editorials and commentaries. They often do not engage in the debate as effectively as on the "Op. Ed." page because they typically express only one opinion, commend only one course of action. Because most citizens do not see competing opinions from competing news editorial sources, indoctrination is as likely a result of editorializing as is education.

Indeed, there are good reasons to believe that we might just as well do without editorials altogether. Paul Neely (1985, pp. 16-17), managing editor of the Chattanooga *Times*, claims that editorials are outdated and arrogant, that they color the paper and undermine credibility.

I am not suggesting that we throw opinion out of the newspaper. There's so much to be said for thoughtful, well-written local opinion. I do suggest that we get rid of the two-column temple of the newspaper's holy word. Many editorial writers have provocative personal opinions. Let's present them as what they are—their opinions, not the collective wisdom of the newspaper.

Let's hire local opinion writers the way the better among us select syndicated columnists, for variety rather than conformity and for originality rather than repetition.

Let's add a healthy habit of actively soliciting opinion from knowledge-able outsiders.

At best, let's develop such a mix of opinion that readers cannot guess how the owners or management of the newspaper stand on any given subject. Let's publish opinion pages of such excellence and such diversity that readers believe there is no concerted effort to sway their thoughts in our direction. (pp. 16-17)

Neely is on target regarding the "educational function" of the news media. We need to find better ways of promoting public debate. Improve-ment is possible by assuring a wider variety of opinion and ideas on any given subject. Also, we can expand the selection of subjects addressed. We could do better in assuring that special points of view held by minorities and women are fully represented. Those changes will be possible when we commit more fully and knowledgeably to performing the educa-tional function.

THE MIRRORING ROLE

Much of what we read in newspapers and hear on news broadcasts seems obviously important but does not fit neatly into either of the above functions. Consider the story about a survivor of a plane crash in the Yukon. Our knowledge about that set of events is not of political significance. Nor is it "educational" in the special sense that I have described above. It is an important story, however, not merely because it is interesting but because it reflects for us something of the human condition. It "mirrors" life. So would the story about the tragedy of the victim who did not survive the same crash.

These stories can have any number of effects on us, of course. They might usefully remind us of the fragility of life, evoke in us a deepened sense of compassion, or cause us to reflect on the human attributes and skills that enable survival under hostile conditions. They are stories we read because we are interested in them, we find them intriguing. Why? Because we have built into ourselves a need to reflect on the fragility of life, to have compassion, and so on. They are more than mere entertainment, and that is why they belong in the news columns and not in the "Style" section.

Stories of tragedy and heroism point to an important aspect of our lives. The story of the volunteer rescuer who risked his life in order to pull people out of the Potomac River, for example, shows that a willingness to risk oneself for the benefit of another is not dead. It gives us a hero to admire and perhaps to emulate. Thus it functions to keep alive just that willingness to risk for others. Such stories show what we are as a people, and perhaps influence what we may become.

A story about the shooting of four would-be teenage robbers in a New York subway is a story we need to know, not because of its political importance only (though it might create sufficient public stir to prompt government action toward subway violence) but because it reflects a significant reality of modern urban life. It is important too because of the issues it raises. Should we outlaw handguns? Under what conditions is violent self-defense justifiable? How can we determine accurately in concrete cases who is the victim and who is the aggressor? It shows us how human beings sometimes respond to threat, real or perceived. The story mirrors life.

It is in part through our collective or common knowledge of such human interest stories that our social ethos emerges. Their stories become part of the lore of our civilization, and that aids in helping us to become one people. It tends toward the creation of community, not just community of knowledge but community in the sense of sharing the world together.

We should exercise caution in deciding which stories to tell. No one can reasonably argue that because we need human interest stories, every particular one should be told. The general need does not supply the compelling imperative for publishing specific stories. There are good reasons sometimes not to publish good stories, even a "hell-uv-a-good story." Sometimes they invade privacy. Sometimes they may embarrass or hurt the innocent.

Indeed, the extensive publicity given to the Potomac River rescuer is a case in point. Shortly after the Air Florida jet crashed into Washington, D.C.'s, 14th Street Bridge, a citizen leaped into the water and helped rescue survivors of the crash. Reporters hounded him for weeks and wrote story after story, ad nauseum. That much limelight destroyed his privacy, at least temporarily. Thus, although it is important that we hear good stories, the fact that a particular story is good does not provide sufficient warrant for its publication, or especially that it be told endlessly.

But why should journalists take on the responsibility of reporting such stories? After all, other agents would spread word of this kind of story. They used to be told over the fence, at the party, in church, and at Rotary. They are still told there. Poets and songwriters tell them. Why should they be in the newsroom?

Part of the answer lies in the fact that news people are the occupational group best equipped to tell them. Journalists are experienced storytellers. Their special talent places on them special responsibilities. (An analogous argument is that of the several people standing around an injured person on the highway, it is the doctor present who has primary duty to render aid.) Moreover, journalists are the ones with most immediate access to the airwaves and newsprint. They have the audiences and can tell the story most widely most quickly.

Just how widely should they be told? We should not ignore the social importance of circulating these "mirroring" stories not merely locally but nationally. Our civilization is composed of a number of ethnic groups. Our customs and habits are different. Attitudes in Maine are unlike those in Texas in significant ways. And yet we are one, bound together with a common future. We govern ourselves by shared laws. For those reasons we need to enrich our common heritage, to know what others are doing (or not doing) and why. We need to see our common life reflected clearly in somebody's mirror.

Perhaps it is worth noting that because our common humanity transcends national boundaries, we should be well served by telling these stories globally. What would the world become if on both sides of the Iron Curtain we knew about and admired each other's heroes!

THE BULLETIN BOARD ROLE

In one respect the press functions like the electric company, as a utility. It is simply the most efficient way we have of making announcements. We announce meeting times and places, births, deaths, marriages, weather, traffic patterns, and that Aunt Minnie's garden won "Garden-of-the-Month." These are things we need very badly to know. They make daily life better, simpler, safer, more comfortable, and often more enjoyable.

My students are wont to claim that the reporter flying around the city in the traffic helicopter is not a "real journalist." But the fact of the matter is that the traffic reporter can give us some very useful information that may have immediate and direct impact on our decisions. I may even get home to dinner on time if at Exit 51 I know that the interstate is blocked this side of Exit 52. And if I had listened more carefully to the weather report, I might have had my raincoat with me and could have arrived at the office dry! These are small matters, to be sure, but they are collectively important in simply living the daily life. They are not glamorous and intrinsically exciting, but they are useful and do make a difference. We legitimately may look to journalists to be the conduit through which these bits of information come to us.

SO WHAT?

The purpose of this essay was from the beginning to "work toward a definition of press responsibility." No full-blown definition has emerged, nor should it. Definitions tend to be static and therefore inadequate for understanding the dynamic interaction between the news media and the public they serve. And even if we had a fully adequate understanding on paper, responsibility for implementing it could not be merely "assigned" to the press. Journalists' responsibilities to society are "contracted" or "self-imposed." That means that the essential concern for journalists and scholars should be the intellectual process of reflecting on the subject, of working toward a definition.

Journalists must make their own determination about their responsibilities. That can happen best through the interchange of ideas, opinions, and ideals about the press both within the newsroom and with thoughtful people outside. With those on the outside the terms of the press-society "covenant" (contracted responsibility) can be hammered out—never fully codified but more fully understood. Reflection within the newsroom is prerequisite to serious assessment of the responsibilities journalists should impose on themselves.

The first step in these processes, it seems to me, should be a reexamination of the socially important functions the press might perform. What functions may society legitimately expect journalists to perform? What ought the serious journalist accept responsibility for doing? The four functions identified here can serve as a beginning for a more sophisticated debate on press responsibility. It is not sufficient to answer, "Publish the news."

REFERENCES

American Bar Association. (1980). *Model code of professional responsibility. Washington, DC: Author.*

Mill, J. S. (1951). Of the liberty of thought and discussion. In *On Liberty* (pp. 102-152). New York: E. P. Dutton, Everyman Ed.

Modern Media Institute. (1983). *The adversary press.* St. Petersburg: Modern Media Institute.

Neely, P. (1985, June). It's time to get rid of editorials: they damage credibility. *ASNE Bulletin. American Society of Newspaper Editors,* pp. 16-17.

2

FOUNDATIONS FOR
NEWS MEDIA RESPONSIBILITY

Deni Elliott

Ask any group of journalists or journalism educators to identify news media responsibilities and they will provide a seemingly contradictory list. Among other things, journalists are said to have responsibilities

(1) to be honest and fair in their presentation of the news,
(2) to speak for the downtrodden,
(3) to get "the story" at all costs,
(4) to serve as the audience's eyes and ears,
(5) to be sensitive to the needs of individuals who become story subjects or sources,
(6) to be a watchdog on government, and
(7) to do whatever each journalist decides is right for him- or herself.

One way to work through these seeming contradictions is to look behind specific "shoulds" and consider how any obligations for the press can be justified. Here, I discuss some philosophical foundations for press action and illustrate that the obligations are not contradictory when one clarifies their foundations.

I argue that journalists have responsibilities that

(1) are based on the function news media have in society,
(2) follow from how specific news organizations define their roles within the communities they serve, and
(3) follow from the individual journalist's own value system.

The word "responsibility" is used here in a conventional way—to mean obligation. A person who does not meet a responsibility is morally blameworthy; that person has done something "wrong."

Describing an action as right or wrong is different from considering whether or not a person is called into account for the behavior. Indeed, some actions might be "wrong" whether the individual committing the action is ever discovered. Torture or murder of innocent persons might be examples of objectively "wrong" actions, at least in a prima facie sense. Whether or not one should be held accountable for failing to meet a responsibility, and the many extralegal ways that journalists are held accountable for their actions, are beyond the scope of this chapter.

The first two categories of responsibilities set limitations on what should be judged as acceptable behavior for journalists within a particular group. In the first category, for example, I discuss responsibilities that apply to all news purveyors in any society. From the second category, I derive responsibilities that limit acceptable behavior for U.S. journalists in particular. These two categories define universal principles—all journalists within the group are morally bound to behave in ways that conform to these principles.

The third category of responsibilities reflects limits that can be set only by the individual journalist. It follows from this addition of personal freedom of choice that there will be a plurality of morally permissible behaviors within the limitations set by the first two categories.

The combination I propose of binding limitations and a variety of acceptable behaviors within those limits is not contradictory. Law, for example, sets limits for permissible behavior, but individuals choose among a great variety of behaviors within that "permissible" scope. Decisions about whether or not to participate in organized religion, about whether or not to have children, about whether or not to vote or to participate in civic affairs exemplify some of the decisions that are based on an individual's own value system. Decisions about whether or not to lie to friends are based on individual morality although we are concurrently bound by law not to lie under oath or to the IRS.

CATEGORY I: RESPONSIBILITY
OF MEDIA TO SOCIETY

Mass media have responsibility to society, no matter what society they may be operating in. Every mass communication system has responsibility to the group of persons who depend on media for messages. This responsibility holds whether the media are privately or governmentally owned, whether or not the controlling news judgments are made within the news organization itself or by an outside agency.

Specifically, any communication organ in any society that is maintained to pass information to a broad and relatively undifferentiated audience of "citizens" has an institutional obligation to tell the readers / listeners what their society expects of them and to tell members of the audience what they can expect from society.[1] I am intentionally excluding narrow-scoped publications such as those written for a defined subculture (business publications, those intended for ethnic groups, political activists, or church members) and those publications, which by decree or custom, are supplementary rather than primary sources of information.[2]

However, assuming that the responsibility laid out for primary information givers is correct (it will be discussed in greater detail soon), how news media actually meet that responsibility may look different from society to society. Before we look specifically at the media, consider that a single guiding principle may look very different as it is interpreted in different situations. For example, assume for a moment that there were a guiding cross-cultural principle that adult children should care for their aging parents. In some cultures, that might mean nursing homes; in others, it might mean having many generations living in the same household; in still other cultures, it might mean that adult children have an obligation to arrange for an easy death for these no longer productive citizens. The same "universal" directive could look different under different circumstances.

In a similar sense, in very restrictive societies, media might well meet this responsibility without performing as we would expect the U.S. news media to act in our very permissive society. For example, the German press during World War II suppressed information concerning bombing missions within the country, but it did let the citizens know that specific cities could no longer be reached by train. This tightly controlled press concealed particulars about the war effort, but it did let people know that their ration coupons were worth less.

The responsibility of "letting readers / listeners know what they can expect from society and what society expects from them" has a broader interpretation in less restrictive cultures. The U.S. press perception of its "responsibility to society" is often coupled with a historically based value of giving the audience as much information as possible about the workings of their local, state, and federal governments.

U.S. media function in a society where citizens both expect and are expected to know what their government is doing. U.S. journalists agree that they have an obligation to provide this information whether they call it "serving as a watchdog on government," "representing the people," "educating the public," "serving the public's right to know," or merely "contributing information and opinions for the public discussion."

Editors and news directors do not agonize over whether or not to carry information about the presidential tax proposal. Although they may not discuss it in "ethical" terms, in some sense they know that they would be irresponsible if they did not provide that information for their audiences.

POWER AS A FOUNDATION FOR SOCIETAL OBLIGATION

I have provided examples of the media meeting their societal responsibility, and will now provide moral justification for why they should meet this responsibility as well. Telling members of the audience what society expects of them and what they can expect from their society is a very powerful function. News media should tell people what they need to know because media have the power to affect the lives of individuals and groups within society. Whether or not citizens like it, whether or not they accept uncritically what is provided by the media, they are dependent upon the news media for vital information.

The media do not constitute an elected power and, admittedly, few individual reporters or editors are ever straightforwardly asked if they wish to hold that power. Nevertheless, news media representatives cannot escape the responsibilities associated with power.

Power entails duties to recognize the dependency of other people and to use power in a judicious manner. Philosophers from Plato forward have argued that no matter how particular persons come to have power within society, they have an obligation to act in a way that is in the interest of the people whom they affect. For example, Plato (1981, 513-514, p. 126) was speaking directly to the mass communicators of his time when he said,

Ought we not then to set about treatment of the state and its citizens on this principle, with the idea of making citizens themselves as good as possible? Without such a principle, as we discovered earlier, one can do no good; no other service to the state is of the slightest avail if those who are to acquire riches or authority over people or any other kind of power are not men of good will.

The most complete arguments for judicious use of power come from philosophers discussing those who govern in society. Of course, philosophers have not agreed throughout history just how these responsibilities should be played out. There is, however, agreement that institutions or people have power to affect the lives of individuals, and that fact entails obligations to use that power in a way that is in the interest of the people they affect.

Although speaking of government in his original piece, John Locke (1973, p. 224), for example, might have been arguing for the prosecution at a contemporary libel trial, pleading for more circumspect use of media power, when he wrote,

> For when the people are made miserable, and find themselves exposed to the ill usage of arbitrary power, cry up their governors as much as you will for sons of Jupiter, let them be sacred and divine, descended or authorized from Heaven; give them out for whom or what you please, the same will happen. The people generally ill treated, and contrary to right, will be ready upon that occasion to ease themselves of a burden that sits heavy upon them.

Even John Stuart Mill, the champion for liberty of speech and the press, has arguments concerning powerful government that can easily be made analogous to the also powerful media. He was arguing that the press serves as a control over powerful government, but his warnings ought to be heeded when one considers mass media as powerful as well. He writes,

> To decide what opinions shall be permitted and what prohibited, is to choose opinions for the people: since they cannot adopt opinions which are not suffered to be presented to their minds. Whoever chooses opinions for the people, possesses absolute control over their actions, and may wield them for his own purposes with perfect security. (Mill, 1976, pp. 148-149)

One may argue that the media constitute a less centralized power than government. Although this may be true on a U.S. national level, it is certainly not the case in the more than 90% of U.S. cities served locally by one mass information purveyor. There, the news organization does, indeed, decide "what opinions shall be permitted and what prohibited" through the making of "news" judgments. Editors and reporters decide what is important and relevant in a news story and what events and issues are worthy of public attention.

Most news organizations, those producing newspapers in particular, do provide some limited audience access through letters to the editor, guest editorials, and free-lance writing. However, that expression is, again, controlled by the news organization. I am not suggesting that most news organizations misuse their power; I am just establishing that they do, indeed, possess great power within society.

There is, of course, an essential difference between how that power is implicit in government and how it is implicit in mass media. Governments govern; media communicate. Yet, whatever the source or manner for institutional power, justice entails a utilitarian directive. Powerful institutions should contribute to the public good. They should not harm individuals or groups within society unless that is necessary for the larger good.

SUMMARY AND DISCUSSION OF
CATEGORY I RESPONSIBILITIES

Within Category I, news media may be said to have obligations to provide information and to strive to cause no harm. Obviously, these two obligations may themselves come into conflict. Providing information may well cause irreparable harm to an individual. But, if the readers/viewers need that information to fulfill their societal expectations, as with information that would affect voting behavior, trust in local government, or understanding of the judicial process, then utilitarian precepts allow the harm of one in favor of the benefit of many.

The responsibilities that come from the function of media and society do not define a complete set of responsibilities for news media in U.S.

society. With only the responsibilities to tell readers/viewers what society expects from them and what they can expect from society, journalists might acceptably deceive both in their information gathering and writing. An additional foundation of responsibility is needed to ensure accuracy and fairness.

CATEGORY II: NEWS ORGANIZATIONS' RESPONSIBILITY TO COMMUNITIES

In addition to the responsibilities that media have to society, news organizations incur obligations relevant to their moment in history, to the communities they serve, and to their professional colleagues. This second set of responsibilities is based on implicit and explicit promises made by the organization.

News organizations in the United States, at least, establish policies that govern behavior, letting the audience and advertisers know what they can expect and letting new employees know what is expected of them. This is done through formal written philosophies, through promotional material directed at audience or advertisers, or simply through day-to-day practice.

Communicating expectations that the news organization is willing to fulfill states promises of sorts. For example, when a news organization says that it offers "all the news that's fit to print," or "all you need to get through your busy day," the organization had better come through with just that.

Although the specific promises may vary slightly from community to community, there are some promises that are consistent throughout U.S. news organizations. For example, virtually all news organizations have promised to provide accurate accounts; they have promised not to lie to the audience. This promise is important to the local community and to a much larger audience as well. Travelers from Boston believe what they read in the Buffalo daily and the one in Boise as well because all U.S. news organizations share a promise to provide accurate accounts. It is because of this promise that news items serve as important documents for researchers. Through the promise made to provide accurate information, the news media serve to document the day's events both for current audiences and posterity.

There is a similar universal promise concerning information gathering. Journalists have an interest in keeping their information gathering above reproach. They owe it to the public trust, certainly, because it is likely that an audience would lose trust in an organization that is shown to be no less corrupt than those it exposes. But, perhaps more important, this is a promise that is owed to other journalists. Just as it is important that the wide U.S. audience trusts all specific news organizations to be as accurate as possible, it is important that the public trust in the profession of journalism be maintained. Information-gathering techniques that lessen public trust are parasitic on journalistic practice and on societal trust in general. If a single journalist or news organization acts in ways that lessen public trust, that journalist subjects all other U.S. journalists to suspicion.

A promise-based category of responsibility implies different obligations from one based on power held by the institutional media. The promise-based category obligates journalists to uphold the public trust in the journalistic craft and to give the audience what they have led readers or viewers to believe they will provide. News organizations have made moral contracts—promises—to provide accurate material of interest and importance.

The promise made by news organizations is essentially no different from the promise made by manufacturers who say that they will provide products that meet certain needs, or from promises made by a neighbor vowing to support another in civic action. Philosopher Charles Fried (1981, p. 8) explains the basis for and moral importance of promises:

> It was a crucial moral discovery that free men [and women] may yet freely serve each others' purposes; the discovery that beyond the fear of reprisal or the hope of reciprocal favor, morality itself might be enlisted to assure not only that you respect me and mine but that you actively serve my purposes. When my confidence in your assistance derives from my conviction that you will do what is right (not just what is prudent), then I trust you and trust becomes a powerful tool for our working our mutual wills in the world. . . .

> The device that gives trust its sharpest, most palpable form is promise. By promising we put in another man's [or woman's] hands a new power to accomplish his [or her] will, though only a moral power: What he [or she] sought to do alone he [or she] may now expect to do with our promised help, and to give him [or her] this new facility was our very purpose in promising. By promising, we transform a choice that was morally neutral into one that is morally compelled.

Editors and reporters sometimes have a hard time accepting that they have "morally compelled" promise-based responsibilities because they, individually and consciously, did not make any such explicit promises. However, in making the free choice to join an established news organization, journalists do implicitly accept the policies and standards of the company. Employees make contracts to do the company's work. Doing the company's work, for a journalist, means carrying out the promises that the news organization has made to the community.

Editors and reporters have an obligation to keep the promises that their news organization makes and to ensure that the organization is keeping its promises in a broad sense. News organizations have promised, in some way, to tell the audience what they will be interested in and to alert readers and viewers to items that they should know about. Some of these items may be clearly defined "events"—announcements of governmental budget, the hiring of a new school superintendent, the fire at a local factory—but other items of importance are "issues" rather than "events."

This is an area where many news organizations have failed to live up to their promise. Part of the obligation to tell readers and listeners about things they should know about includes informing them about developing issues and social conflicts before these become explosive events. It also means keeping important issues before the public after explosive events would otherwise be forgotten.

The covering of demonstrations by minority groups provides a good example of this issue/event problem, and is addressed in great detail in Chapter 7. There is no argument that the confrontations themselves constitute news, but when considering the need for public discussion and U.S. citizen input on social reform, the issues underlying the events are even more important. However, the issues themselves are rarely discussed in mass market news publications prior to an explosive event; they are often disregarded by journalists soon after public confrontation has ended. In failing to keep significant issues on the public agenda, new organizations are failing to keep an important promise.

THE TWO COMPLEMENTARY CATEGORIES
OF RESPONSIBILITY

The second category of responsibility supplements the first. Based on the two categories, U.S. journalists are obligated to do the following:

(1) tell people what they can expect from society and what society expects from them,

(2) do so in a way that avoids causing unnecessary harm,

(3) tell people what is and what should be of interest to them, and

(4) do so in a way that will not lessen public trust in the profession of journalism.

Consider the responsibilities listed at the beginning of this essay, and it is clear that attempting to meet a variety of journalistic obligations does not present a paradox. Based on Category I responsibilities, journalists are obliged to be sensitive to the needs of individuals who become story subjects and sources, to serve as a watchdog on government, to get the story at all costs, and to be the eyes and ears for their audience. Based on the usual promises made by U.S. news organizations, journalists also have responsibilities to be honest and fair in their presentation, and to speak for the downtrodden (in that it is important for readers and viewers to know about the "downtrodden" of the community).

As will be discussed soon, individual journalists also have a complementary responsibility to do whatever they decide is right.

Of course, the responsibilities often appear to be in conflict with one another. Just as the responsibility to give readers information may compete with doing no harm, keeping promises may compete with the functional responsibilities. Taking a relatively easy case, news organizations routinely withhold information from their readers during kidnappings or other situations in which an individual's life is at stake. Certainly, the readers are interested in knowing as much as they can about the situation, but preventing harm to the victim does and should take precedence. The journalists set aside their promise to share accurate information with the audience in order to prevent harm. And, they do so knowing that reasonable members of the audience would understand and applaud their decision.

The kidnapping case demonstrates the priority of Category I responsibilities over those in Category II. When responsibilities from the two categories compete, those based on function and power have prima facie weight. The promise-based responsibilities are not reducible to those that are power-based, but news organizations could not make and carry out promises unless they were first meeting their functional responsibilities.

CATEGORY III: RESPONSIBILITY TO SELF

Clearly, the individual journalist is obligated to carry out the responsibilities discussed above. Reporters and editors implicitly agree to carry out these responsibilities by calling themselves journalists and taking jobs at established news organizations.

However, journalists are more than representatives of the media and more than representatives of specific news organizations. First, they are each autonomous moral agents, and thus responsible for their own actions. Illustrations abound to show that a person cannot hide from personal responsibility by attributing his or her action to a supervisor's directive. Individuals are morally blameworthy for their wrong actions even if they were following another's directions in performing the acts. "My editor told me to do it" is not justification for one's action; nor is, "That's just what journalists do."

Because individuals are blameworthy (and praiseworthy) for their actions, it is vital that journalists be consciously aware of their own moral beliefs. Individual value systems or beliefs can serve as a check on conventional "professional" dictates that serve no larger purpose for the community—on the journalistic norms that are not justifiable on the promise or power base. For example, "Never let your source see a news story prior to publication" is a journalistic convention operative in most U.S. newsrooms. Yet, more than one thoughtful journalist has set this convention aside when working on specific stories because they decide, in an autonomous fashion, that accuracy in a complex story or fairness to a source demands otherwise.

However, even if individuals are able to identify that their "gut" tells them that conventional wisdom is not acceptable in particular cases, they may not be able to articulate the just why they hold certain beliefs. In a pragmatic sense, a deep sense of self-knowledge is not necessary. The bases upon which individuals develop value systems are unique and complex combinations of religious beliefs, education, family and cultural norms, individual rationality, and consciously or unconsciously accepted conventions of the many subcultures in which one lives. The basic responsibility to self—what is important for autonomous moral agency—is an individual's ability to identify, express, and follow through on his or her convictions.

Individual autonomy is necessary for the moral health of any profession or group. A plurality of value systems among practitioners is acceptable and even preferred over uniform beliefs. Conventional norms that define group behavior change only through friction. If all members of a professional group shared exactly the same values, there would be no hope for improvement or growth, no questioning of normative attitudes or actions. Acceptable values change over time. For example, accepting free gifts and handouts, once considered bonuses of the job, is now grounds for being fired in most news organizations. Individual journalists decided that taking "freebies" compromised their ability to perform their jobs dispassionately.

Journalists also have a responsibility to the ideas of tolerance and plurality that allow them to operate with autonomous values. This implies that journalists should welcome diverse approaches and not judge other journalists' actions against a personal belief system.

That is different, however, from saying that anything goes for journalists. Each autonomous moral agent must decide what is correct action for him- or herself, but those choices must be made within an understanding of the responsibilities inherent to the profession. Perhaps the first way that the obligation for journalists to "do whatever he or she decides is right" plays out is in the individual's career decision. Individuals choose to take on responsibilities associated with the profession in the same way that one chooses to become a member of a church, civic, or social group. Once on the job, the journalist operates autonomously, but within justifiable limitations. The proper criteria against which to judge individual journalistic actions are the responsibilities that are based on the industry's power and promises.

The point of this chapter has been to establish the foundations from which one can derive journalistic obligations. The power-based and promise-based foundations serve as bases from which to derive obligations that are essential for journalists to accept. These foundations also serve as criteria against which one can judge journalistic practices to determine which practices reflect professional obligations and which are merely norms.

With the addition of Category III, we see that journalists are indeed autonomous, operating as freely as the Constitution writers intended. Operating freely includes voluntarily embracing the responsibilities to society and community that are inherent in one's profession choice.

NOTES

1. I am indebted to Professor George Reedy of Marquette University who formulated the institutional responsibility in these words in personal conversation in 1983.

2. I understand that there is a definitional problem here. Some may argue that citizens of any particular society necessarily share some worldview. It is impossible to escape the fact, for example, that "accept a plurality of world views" is, itself, a U.S. worldview. Where does one draw the line between a mass market newspaper, which is based on the assumption that the broad community audience has an understanding and some degree of acceptance of U.S. values, and the special interest publication that lets revisionist subscribers know how their particular political goals are being reached or undermined? I concede that that line is sometimes difficult to draw. However, for purposes of this discussion, I assume that, without having a clear definition, most individuals could quickly identify mass market news publications and radio and television news programs within other media offerings.

REFERENCES

Fried, C. (1981). *Contract as promise*. Cambridge, MA: Harvard University Press.
Locke, J. (1973). Second treatise on civil government. In J. C. King & J. A. McGilvray (Eds.), *Political and social philosophy, traditional and contemporary readings*. New York: McGraw-Hill.
Mill, J. S. (1976). Law of libel and liberty of the press. In G. Williams (Ed.), *John Stuart Mill on politics and society*. New York: International Publications Service (Harvester Press Limited).
Plato, (1981). *Gorgias* (W. Hamilton, Trans.). New York: Penguin.

PART II

Responsibility and Press Theory

Theories of journalistic responsibility do not exist in an vacuum.
Philosophical theories, such as those presented in Part I, complement
or compete with press, political, and legal theories. In Part II, the
authors examine questions of journalistic responsibility within the
context of these other theories. They arrive at very different answers.

All five chapters in this section address the question, "How should
responsible journalists act?"

In Chapter 3, Merrill argues that journalists act responsibly only
when they are each acting as they each want. No responsibility should
be imposed by government, audience, or even by the institutional
media.

In the next chapter, Barney concludes that journalists are acting
responsibly when they are consciously presenting as many alternative
opinions to the public as possible. While the content should be
varied, journalists should share an intent to present a broad range of
views.

In Chapter 5, Glasser makes the case that journalists should act in
the public's interest rather than in their own.

Dennis states, in Chapter 6, that responsible journalism is
journalism that is representative of the citizens.

In the last chapter in Part II, Christians argues that journalists are
acting responsibly when they are speaking for the voiceless in society.

The authors are just as divided on the question, "Why should
journalists act responsibly?"

Merrill answers that our whole notion of democracy depends on
journalists being free to act as they wish, even if their actions are seen
as irresponsible by some.

Barney argues that democracy depends on a plurality of messages and viewpoints, thus journalists ought to be committed to presenting alternative views.

Glasser says that an affirmative reading of the First Amendment makes it clear that that amendment was designed to protect public interest, not media owners, and that government should step in to make sure that freedom of the press is protected from private as well as public abuse.

Dennis concludes that the press should act responsibly because representation is part of media function. However, he makes it clear that much discussion is needed on the notion of representation before that responsibility can be clearly defined.

Christians argues that journalists should speak for the voiceless in society because media have a clear responsibility to present a representative picture of all of society. It is the oppressed who are often not seen and not heard through the institutional media.

There is no effort here to reconcile these conflicting points of view. The views of the authors constitute the broad range of arguments that come up when journalists or academicians consider how the notion of responsibility fits with theories of the press. While no one author would accept the arguments presented in this section as equally correct or acceptable, they all do value the conflicting points of view. The process of working toward the "correct" view is perhaps even more important for a democratic press than ever reaching an answer. In this way, media theory models for society what discussion on vital issues ought to be about.

3

THREE THEORIES OF PRESS RESPONSIBILITY AND THE ADVANTAGES OF PLURALISTIC INDIVIDUALISM

John C. Merrill

Prescriptive and proscriptive rhetoric abounds today in the area of press responsibility—admonitions, directions, guidelines, prohibitions, and denunciations. Increasingly, such rhetoric is being formalized in codes of ethics, but largely it comes upon us in a plethora of unsystematized papers, articles, and books. And, of course, hardly a serious conversation is held among journalists and other communication specialists in which the subject of press or media responsibility does not come up.

Increasingly, the thrust of such rhetoric is that the press is not very ethical—that it is not being responsible to society. In addition, it is claimed that the press appears to be getting worse (more irresponsible) and that something needs to be done about it.

We hear such lamentations on the local level, the national level, and, since about 1970, even on the international level. Such press criticism emanates from both ideological liberals and conservatives. It comes in the form of isolated bombasts, in institutionalized declarations from professional and learned societies, from sensitive politicians, cynical academics, and from the so-called average citizen who is fed up with press excesses. We hear it from Republicans and Democrats, socialists and capitalists, rich and poor—and, even more frequently, from journalists themselves.

Everyone seems to be out to define what "responsible" journalism is. Listen to Clark Mollenhoff (1964), long-time Washington correspondent:

> The future of the American Democracy is contingent upon the performance of the American press. If the newsmen of today and tomorrow are

diligent workers and balanced thinkers on problems of governing our
society, then I have no doubt that the American Democracy will survive
and flourish as a symbol to the whole world. If the press fails in its
responsibility—if it founders in a quagmire of superficiality, partisanship,
laziness and incompetence—then our great experiment in democracy will
fail.

We are told here that if democracy fails, it is the fault of the American
press. If our democracy fails, it means that the press has been
"superficial, partisan, lazy and incompetent." Why, we might ask, has
not our democracy already failed, for certainly many feel the press has
been all of these things? And certainly, parts of the press have been—at
least in somebody's opinion.

Those who say that the U.S. press is "irresponsible" are seeing in it
some real or imaginary danger to the national society or public
interest—or to those aspects of the society that appear to these critics as
most important. Those who might view the press of the USSR or the
Philippines as irresponsible would do so if in their views the press was
exhibiting mannerisms that endangered the equilibrium and ongoing of
their respective national societies. Responsibility and irresponsibility
are not only relative to the particular society under consideration, but
even within an individual society the terms have a multitude of meanings
depending on the degree of pluralism present.

No shortage of responsibility definers and dictators exists today, and
there has never been a shortage. Press libertarians such as James and
John Stuart Mill evidenced the schizophrenia—supporting freedom but
dictating its terms—prevalent in this whole area. James Mill, perhaps
the first proponent of the "watchdog function" of journalism, advocated
press freedom because it "made known the conduct of the individuals
who have been chosen to wield the powers of government" (Zashin,
1972, p. 25). This is the dilemma (a hypothetical imperative in the
Kantian sense): circumscribing the conditions for a free press. Would
James Mill have canceled liberty of the press for those press units that
failed to live up to his rationale for such freedom? We don't know, but
presumably he would have.

John Stuart Mill, James's son, wanted to hold the individual to a high
standard of responsibility to his fellow men, but he was a freedom lover
to the extent that he did prefer that "the conscience of the agent himself"
enforce a person's responsibility and that a free society should put few
restrictions on its members' behavior (Zashin, 1972, p. 49). And, again,

if the agent's conscience did not enforce the person's responsibility as Mill saw it, then what?

The remainder of this chapter could be taken up with a recounting of those persons who have proposed duties and responsibilities for the press. Hardly a person writes or talks about the press without setting for it a set of responsibilities. Most of these responsibility definers like to project their opinions, to universalize, to go beyond simply having an opinion. In short, they are manifesting not only a certain arrogance but also something of the spirit of authoritarianism, however well-meaning they may be. This idea is developed extensively elsewhere (Merrill, 1974).

In the face of all the criticism of the press, and in view of the multitudes of responsibility definers among us, we are left with the problem of finding the best way to arrive at a state of press responsibility. First, let me propose three main approbative theories of press responsibility, and then we shall consider their strengths and weaknesses.

The three press responsibility theories are as follows:

(1) That which is legally defined or determined by government;
(2) That which is professionally defined or determined by the press itself;
(3) That which is pluralistically defined or determined by the individual journalists themselves.

The thesis of this chapter is that the last theory—responsibility as individually defined—is the valid one, the meaningful one for our society, and that any other concept of press responsibility would be incongruent with our ideology, our constitution, our tradition, and our concern for a pluralistic society. In other words, I am maintaining that the third theory is the only one that is really harmonic with our social values and goals and, in spite of individual instances of questionable journalistic behavior in the press system, permits the greatest potential for freedom and responsibility. It is, in short, for the United States, the superior one of the three macrotheories of press responsibility.

Americans could, of course, accept the first theory—having the press conform to a legal concept of press responsibility. But this would seem to be a direct affront to the First Amendment; therefore, largely, but perhaps not entirely, it has to be set aside. Of course, the press in one sense, would be more "responsible" if some type of governmental (judicial) supervision came about; sensational material could be controlled in the press, and government activities could always be supported and public policy could be championed.

Under the governmental-level approach to responsibility the press could be more "educational" in the sense that less sensational news would appear, whereas more news of art exhibits, concerts, speeches by government personages, and national progress in general could be emphasized. In short, the press would stress the positive and eliminate, or minimize, the negative. Then, with one voice, the press of the nation would be responsible to its society (at least from the governmental perspective); and the definition of "responsible journalism" would be functional in a monolithic way—defined by the courts and monitored by functionaries of the government.

In spite of the "neatness" and basic appeal of Theory 1, it is the second theory (professionally defined responsibility) that seems to be gaining popularity in the United States. Certainly it is more enticing constitutionally and it does not smack so obviously of incipient authoritarianism. The government would not be involved, yet there would be a kind of enforcement mechanism—in this case, all the professional selectivity and control normally found in exclusive, paradigmatic professions.

Large numbers of press people want to be, and are, on the road to professionalism today. In spite of its basic appeal for journalists, professionalization has some obvious dangers and other journalists are cautious of proceeding too rapidly in that direction.

A profession is selective and exclusive; it has minimum entrance requirements; it has an elite directorate who can eliminate "irresponsible" members; it has a code of ethics to direct its members, and it has some kind of certification or licensing system. Professionalizing in this sense may work well for medicine and law, to name two, but journalists—or some of them—see journalism as somewhat different. Because journalism has no discrete body of knowledge, and because "freedom of the press" implies to many the freedom to be a journalist, and because licensing would work to restrict much-valued pluralism and contentiousness in American journalism, there is a reluctance to embrace professionalization too quickly and without considerable thought and concern.

So, it seems that "legal" responsibility, with its anti-First Amendment overtones, is not really an acceptable option. Neither really is "professional" responsibility, although the drift appears to be toward an ultimate embracing of this theory. Both theories pose problems for basic press freedoms. This leaves us with Theory 3 (the pluralistically defined responsibility concept)—not perfect, of course, but seemingly more consistent with American ideology and tradition than the other two. The objective is, as it has been from J. S. Mill onward, to permit individual and independent editorial determinism, trying all the while to raise journalistic moral consciousness through sound education and competitive persuasion.

Keeping in mind the three approbative theories just taken up, let us consider the whole question of press responsibility a little further.

In 1984 military forces of the United States went to the island of Grenada in the Caribbean. The press was not permitted to land with the troops and to cover the initial phases of the operation there. By and large, the American press was enraged: How could the press be responsible to its society if it could not provide coverage? But the majority of Americans felt that the press should not have gone in with the troops—that it could *not* have been responsible had it done so.

Here we are confronted with an important question: Who determines responsibility for the society—the government that kept the press out, the journalists who wanted in, or the majority of citizens who sided with the government?

In a free society, it would appear that press responsibility is in the eye of the beholder. If we like press actions, they are responsible; if we do not like press actions, then they are irresponsible.

The Bay of Pigs case also comes to mind. Was the U.S. press responsible during the Kennedy administration in not reporting the Bay of Pigs invasion? Or was it acting irresponsibly, as the *New York Times* concluded, by not reporting it?

It is very strange that Americans generally embrace pluralism and freedom, but at the same time seem to want some type of monolithic press responsibility. These two desires are logically contradictory. What we will have with freedom are some press units thought to be responsible by some segments of the society and others thought to be irresponsible. A mixture of responsible and irresponsible press actions is the logical result of a media system that allows maximum freedom.

Listen to Arthur Ochs Sulzberger, publisher of the *New York Times*, talking about this problem to the staffers of the *Yale Daily News* in late 1984: "It is going to be very important how the press handles itself, for I fear that there is continuing move afoot to cast the American press as untrustworthy and indeed somewhat un-American." He continued, "There seems to be a growing feeling that our free press is not consistently enough a responsible press, and that both regulation and punishment are called for" (Greer, 1984).

Evidently Sulzberger is not enthralled with those who believe that the press "is not consistently enough a responsible press." This would not mean, of course, that Sulzberger is against responsible journalism, but that he is concerned about certain "definers" of responsibility. The publisher wants "responsibility" defined by the individual news decision makers in the press, at least by his decision makers. Certainly he does not want it defined by the national administration or the courts; he says so very clearly. And, back in 1973, he made it clear that he did not even want it defined by a presumably independent body—a press council. He was an outspoken critic and noncooperator with the now-defunct National News Council (Salant, 1984).

Sulzberger's position would seem to be the classic position of American journalism, in spite of the voices one hears more frequently in favor of a less press-oriented definition of press responsibility. More and more there are calls for a responsible press, even if it must be brought about by government or law. Here is the position of Dr. Walter Berns (1974, p. 135), a well-known political scientist:

> Whatever the tension that exists between them, a responsible press need not be the opposite of a free press; and a government that, through its laws, acts to promote a responsible press is not by that fact the opposite of a free government. Not only are such laws not incompatible with free government, they may be a necessary condition for it.

We all would probably agree that a responsible press is preferable to an irresponsible press. Certainly the press should be responsible and I maintain that it is. It is responsible to somebody's concept of responsibility. But many critics say that this is not enough!

Presumably, the press should be responsible to everyone, everyone at the same time. Of course, any reasonable person knows that this is not really possible. Interests conflict. Reportorial perspectives vary. Editorial biases go in different directions. Perceptions by audience members are not the same. What is one person's "responsible journalism" may well be another's "irresponsible journalism."

Of course, Professor Bern's plan of action would remedy this relativism in the responsibility concept. We can have laws that will force all segments of journalism to accept a common concept of journalistic responsibility. And this is very popular with people who sincerely want to see a "better" press and more "responsible" journalism. But, of course, this remedy is extremely difficult in view of the First Amendment's position on such an action. But the First Amendment can be changed, many say, and perhaps it will be one day.

About the only other "remedy" that might be proposed, other than the normal array of pressures on the press such as press councils, critical journalism reviews, letters to the editor, and such, is to raise the consciousness of journalists to a higher moral level where these journalists will voluntarily act more responsibly in accordance with their own ethical principles.

This, of course, is not what the press critics want. For, in a real sense, nothing substantial would really change in the press system with such "volunteerism." Journalists in the United States already have this option: to act responsibly, or to try to, according to their own standards. This is nothing more than the core of libertarianism, a state from which the new press critics and the proponents of social responsibility are trying to lead us.

Many readers will say that such a conclusion is a gross oversimplification. They will contend that they are not necessarily calling for laws to make the press more responsible; they are calling for a kind of professionalization with its trappings of ethical codes, licensing, minimal entrance requirements, and a "de-pressing" mechanism for irresponsible journalists. This would not endanger the provisions of the First Amendment, they say, but would give incentives for the press to act responsibly. If this is what the critics really want, then, as I argue elsewhere (Dennis & Merrill, 1984), they are embracing Theory 2.

As was said earlier, this is a kind of extragovernment option. If we cannot assault the First Amendment by passing laws to guide our irresponsible press, and if we are unwilling to leave the question of responsibility in the hands of individual journalists—which I am proposing in this chapter—then we can possibly achieve a kind of responsibility by making journalism a true profession. Then, the deviant (irresponsible?) journalists can be kept in line (or ejected from the profession) by their peers (and not by government) by forcing them to submit to the definition of "responsibility" proclaimed by the profession.

This professionalization would, in fact, provide a "solution." Forget about laws and forget about a pluralistically defined "responsibility," a kind of individual morality that, according to many ethicists, does not take the social good into consideration. What we would have with a professionalized journalism would be a kind of institutional concept of responsibility, a kind of self-regulation, projected into American journalism. And, therefore, it would be "responsible."

But would it? It would, of course, be responsible in the eyes of the elite core in the profession who formulated it. But would it be responsible to every member of the profession, even if through fear of being de-pressed the members tried to conduct their activities in correspondence to this professional concept?

And, what is probably more important to ask: Would the professional journalistic concept of press responsibility be accepted or supported (and lauded) by the citizens of the country who are the consumers of this "responsible" journalism? In a diversified and opinionated society such as ours, there is no doubt but that there would be considerable disagreement with much of this "socially responsible" journalism defined and practiced by the profession of journalists.

So, are we not back where we started? Responsibility in journalism has returned—as it must surely return in an open society—to the personal and individual definitions of the persons who are concerned with it. And, those persons who are not concerned with it must be controlled, if they are controlled at all, either by law or by professional sanctions. We have already noted the problems with both of these responsibility theories.

Even if a "profession" of journalism develops to the point where it can mandate for its members, for example, that sources of information must always be given (or must not be given), this will not mean that the controversy about responsible journalism will disappear. Even if all journalists conform to certain journalistic standards, the question as to whether what they are doing is "responsible" will still exist in the society. The general rules (and exceptions to them) will in the future, as they have been in the past and are today, have their proponents and opponents. There is no way in a free and open society to settle this question of press responsibility.

A free press will be responsible to some people in some circumstances and to some degree. And, likewise, it will be irresponsible. Some press units will be considered responsible by some and irresponsible by others. And some parts of some press units will be considered both responsible and irresponsible by some persons and groups in the society. There is no way around it, short of authoritarianism where some totalitarian or monolithic concept of responsibility (such as in the USSR) is forced upon the entire press system. This would, of course, pretty well settle the question for the press, but the question would still persist: Is the press "responsible" for the society even if the press acts according to a single standard?

The theory proposed in this chapter (Theory 3) will not eliminate the voices raised against press "irresponsibility" either. Because we have at present Theory 3 underpinning our press system, we know very well that charges of irresponsible journalism are heard from all sides. So, as a theory designed to eliminate differences of opinion about responsibility, the "pluralistically defined" theory is certainly no better than the other two; it may even be considered inferior on this criterion. But, as no theory will prove to be completely satisfactory, Theory 3 does have the advantage of retaining a maximum degree of freedom for the press and assuring greater message and practitioner pluralism than would be possible under the other two theories.

Although societies are getting more complex and institutions are bigger and harder to control, it is too early to rush headlong into collectivistic "solutions" without reconsidering the strengths and advantages of individualistic approaches. In concluding this chapter with its emphasis on individualism, it seems appropriate to quote Friedrich Hayek as he warns against tendencies that would organize or plan or direct intellectual pursuits (and certainly journalism is one such pursuit). He wrote in his classic *The Road to Serfdom* (1944, pp. 165-166):

> It may indeed be said that it is the paradox of all collectivist doctrine and its demand for "conscious" control of "conscious" planning that they necessarily lead to the demand that the mind of some individual should rule supreme—while only the individualistic approach . . . makes us recognize the super-individual forces which guide the growth of reason. Individualism is thus an attitude of humility before this social process and of tolerance to other opinions and is the exact opposite of that intellectual *hubris* which is at the root of the demand for comprehensive direction of the social process.

Hayek has touched the centrality of the nature of individualism— tolerance to other opinions. This is at the root of the theory of pluralistic individualism as it impinges on the concept of press responsibility. By tolerating other opinions (as to even the nature of press responsibility), neither journalistic eccentricity nor press pluralism is discouraged. The result is a theory congruent with the basic (avowed) values and tradition of the American press and society.

One could object to the three approbative theories of responsibility presented here, saying that there are other definers or approvers for press action; for example, individual media managers or employers, and perhaps even general social peer pressure. Another possibility, someone may say, is an approbative theory designated as "theological." It is true that the church or a holy book can have a great impact on a concept of responsibility, but this chapter has ignored these as marginally important in the area of press responsibility. And, of the three theories discussed here, that which is pluralistically defined or determined by the individual journalists seems to have the greatest number of advantages in American society. There has been no contention here that this theory would have such advantages in all societies.

A more compelling objection might be raised against the thesis of this chapter, one that gets back to the subject of ethics and responsibility. Doesn't the advocacy of Theory 3 simply ignore the matter of press ethics and evade the public dissatisfaction with the way segments of the press actually operate? An obvious question. And, an obvious answer is that Theory 3 does appear to ignore, or at least circumvent, any real concern for ethics. But, actually, it does not ignore ethics at all; it simply projects ethics to the individual rather than to a monolithic collectivity. It places the ethical burden on the individual journalist, where it ultimately falls, and seeks through education and voluntary journalistic exposure to moral thinking the progress that is healthy and desirable for free people.

As has been said earlier, and should be stated again in conclusion, the acceptance of (or retention of) Theory 3 will not eliminate criticism of the press or dissatisfaction with its news and editorial decisions. To regulate responsibility in the press (to foster a monolithic concept), a press system must adhere to Theory 1 or to a tightly controlled Theory 2. If we want to preserve freedom while insisting on a more responsible press, then we are really left with Theory 3. If we apply systematic instrumental means in an attempt to gain press responsibility, we run the great danger of losing press freedom.

POSTSCRIPT

Today, many of us "fossilized academics" are an endangered species as the new Critical Theorists make a mad rush to "get beyond" the basic libertarian paradigm and push into socially relevant frontiers where, ostensibly, wider participation in public communication is possible.

In this day when the new critics (taking their intellectual vigor from the Frankfurt School's early concern for alienated audience members, lack of people's self-determination, and a deeply help suspicion of the status quo) are interjecting their Marxist orientations into communications research and criticism, it is almost heresy to reassert the efficacy of classical liberalism—the paradigmatic advantages of press libertarianism.

As I pointed out a decade ago in *The Imperative of Freedom* (1974), the emphasis in main-line academic concern was shifting from the media to the people, from press rights to people's rights. This trend has continued, as I predicted it would, but even faster. It has gained momentum as students of the sixties have found themselves increasingly the young researchers and social critics of the eighties. Institutions, especially capitalistic ones, have become suspect, and empirical researchers are being replaced by critical analysts who are using their ideologies, biases, and passions "to change society." Describing society is no longer enough for them; the essential thing is to have an impact on society. Theory alone is inadequate, they say; it must be tied to practice and to concepts in order to foster social justice. And this pragmatic emphasis at least partially explains why theory and research seem to be enthroning the audiences and dethroning the communicators and media institutions, at least in capitalist countries.

"Media-centered" paradigms are falling on bad times; "audience-centered" paradigms are being championed. Theoretical and research attention is being given to analyzing audience needs, frustrations, alienation, and is given less and less to media-related problems and functions. More attention is placed on audience needs, fears, hopes, and freedoms; concomitant emphasis is now being given to the media's shortcomings, obligations, and duties.

Robert A. White (of London's Centre for the Study of Communication and Culture) has capsulized extremely well the new emphasis, the search for new paradigms, and the growing popularity of Critical Theory. Scholarship must, according to White (1983), give more attention to "authoritarianism" in the media, media linkage with powerful interests, the roles and rights of receivers, the unmasking of self-serving ideologies of the media, and the power and mechanisms of social control in the media.

There is no reason to disagree with White (1983, p. 283) when he says that there is an "increasing interest in participatory communication, demand for public access to media channels, insistence on balancing libertarian rights of the media with the public's right to know, media reform movements, and the spread of education for critical use of media, and the greater appreciation of the value of popular culture." This state of academic concern summarized by White is far more advanced in Europe (and in many places in the Third World) and is, more slowly, making inroads in the United States.

It is quite natural, in view of the tendencies in scholarship just summarized, that a theory of *pluralistic individualism* (with its emphasis on communicators, sources, media) would be outside the main channels of contemporary theorizing. Journalist-centered theories, already weak in 1974 when I wrote *The Imperative of Freedom*, have quickly eroded and so-called audience-centered theories and the concomitant criticism of institutionalized journalism have moved in to replace them.

This trend to depower the press, to limit its freedom, to restrict its options, to denude its agenda-setting potential, to discredit its separation from the state, to minimize its autonomy, to prescribe its social duties, and to tame its aspirations—all in the name of "people's rights"—has made tremendous strides in communication scholarship. Critical Theorists of the 1980s, with their strong ideological proclivities and social agenda, have taken up the banners of the Hutchins Commissioners of the 1940s and are effectively discrediting the Western press and shaking the very foundations of liberal theory.

To a press libertarian, of course, this is rather sad. But there is always hope that the vaunted dialectic of Hegel and Marx will work, even in this area, and that scholars will see the authoritarian and monolithic dangers to self-styled "people's communication" and help to swing future theory back to a "synthesis" position where press freedom is protected and the audience's desires and expectations are realized.

REFERENCES

Berns, W. (1974). Constitution and a responsible press. In H. Clor (Ed.), *The mass media and modern democracy* (pp. 113-135). Chicago: Rand McNally.

Dennis, E., & Merrill, J. C. (1984). Journalism as a profession. *Basic Issues in Mass Communication: A Debate* (pp. 149-160). New York: Macmillan.

Greer, W. R. (1984, November 11). Publisher of Times cites concern for press in second Reagan term. *The New York Times*.

Hayek, F. (1944). *The road to serfdom* (pp. 165-166). Chicago: University of Chicago Press, Phoenix Books.

Merrill, J. C. (1974). *The imperative of freedom*. New York: Hastings House.

Mollenhoff, C. R. (1964, February). *Life line of democracy*. Unpublished paper presented as the 15th Annual William Allen White Memorial Lecture, University of Kansas.

Salant, R. S. (1984, October). The late—or too soon—national news council. *The Journalist* (University of Southern California School of Journalism).

White, R. A. (1983). Mass communication and culture: Transition to a new paradigm. *Journal of Communication, 33*(3), p. 283.

Zashin, E. M. (1972). *Civil disobedience and democracy*. New York: Free Press.

4

THE JOURNALIST AND A
PLURALISTIC SOCIETY:
AN ETHICAL APPROACH

Ralph D. Barney

Social pluralism has often been appauded but seldom explored in the United States—particularly pluralism in journalism or the mass media.

As a result, there has been little effort to define journalistic pluralism or to deal with it as a fundamental necessary characteristic of a participatory democracy. In particular, few dialogues have explored the ethical imperatives in a pluralistic, largely libertarian, society. Yet the ethical imperatives seem extremely important in the light of changing media conditions.

Pluralism assumes particular importance because of recent spectacular growth of professional persuaders (special pleaders) and extensive redistribution of audiences across available mass media.

Special pleaders are a class of professional communicators whose function (public relations or advertising) is to persuade, largely through the media, in a client's favor. These professionals place a large and highly skilled force at the disposal of vested interests in the media mix. They constitute a group of informational mercenaries.

Because the special pleader is most often available to the cause best able to pay, other social forces are needed to provide some informational balance. The pluralistic imperative suggests such a balancing force.

Perhaps a few operational definitions are in order before further consideration can be given to the problems and concepts of pluralism.

Terms such as "participatory society," "right-to-know," "pluralism," and "ethical imperative" elicit vague nods of understanding, but seldom are either discussed or understood. Yet, they should form the bedrock of informed discussion about the direction social communications systems should take. Therefore, in order to help us understand some ethical considerations, let us look for a moment at definitions of a few important social mechanisms.

PARTICIPATORY SOCIETY

A participatory society is one in which the individual member actively participates in determining his or her own destiny. It is a society of discussion, learning, experimentation, and growth.

In the more common "instructional" society, the individual has no incentive or reward for individual self-development. Indeed, such individualism is discouraged and a fairly rigid conformity becomes a goal of socialization.

A participatory society, on the other hand, encourages, and respects, the individual's participation in its rites. In such a society, public opinion is revered as the power that, when expressed with sufficient force, transcends the law. In short, a participatory society owes its good health, and even its very existence, to the participation of a broad cross-section of its citizens in the decision-making process.

An important elementary observation is that society is composed of individuals, each of whom finds it necessary to face each day as it comes. Each is seeking, from whatever source, and from experience, the information necessary to cope with this daily confrontation with reality.

Such a daily exercise in coping necessitates, if one hopes to achieve satisfaction and contentment, a myriad of informed decisions. However small, each of those decisions will have some effect on one's relative happiness. The accumulation of decisions by 240 million Americans each day determines the overall social health of the nation.

These decisions range from the relatively minor (color or style of clothing) to the major (who, or whether, to marry or what job to take in what part of the world) with all gradations between.

A basic assumption in the United States (bolstered by the Bill of Rights and other social supports of a self-determinant society) is that the individual member of the society is capable of making intelligent decisions—harvesting the fruits of the wiser decisions and accepting consequences for less astute choices.

If this is so, the communication climate and the information-gathering systems of individuals are crucial to the national social health. Again, look at how individuals develop.

They construct, based on their own perceptions of their needs, personal communication systems or networks to develop a decision-making mechanism. This improves their survival chances and assists their progress within society. Such a network yields the information that will allow them to function effectively at whatever level of social participation personal choice and capabilities dictate.

This means, for example, that a corporate junior executive who hopes for a meteoric rise in his or her organization should be perceptive enough to develop a complex information system that will be of immense assistance. The system should, if effective, provide the aspiring executive with information needed to anticipate accurately—and therefore exploit—organizational decisions and corporate opportunities.

One who "makes things happen" often acts from an information orientation. That individual encounters informal information within the corporate rumor mill, assesses its accuracy, and then can place him- or herself realistically in the way of opportunity with an informed view of risk/reward ratios. When consistently and wisely done, this increases chances for promotion or success over more passive coworkers.

At the other extreme, a worker with a relatively low ambition level more likely develops a limited system of information contacts—generally those in the area of a special interest or that allow him or her to merely maintain him- or herself in a situation. As a result, the individual displays a greater functional apathy toward information containing seeds of personal progress.

The quality of individuals' lives is going to be determined by (a) their consistent knowledge of available alternatives as they make decisions and (b) their ability to develop the analytical skills that lead to consistently "correct" decisions. Because history ultimately judges whether decisions are correct, the skill often results in guesses rather than surety-based actions. The efficient, purposive information gatherer increases probabilities of correct decisions by gathering more information, lowering the probability of surprise results brought on by ignorance. Judgment skills are a critical factor here, but their role awaits another discussion.

In an evolving information society, the individual is under increasing pressure to express thoughtful opinion, a pressure for which traditional, intimate communication systems may not be adequate. One must, for example, contribute to national decisions about consumption of fossil fuels, gun control, U.S. involvement in Central America, Middle East tensions, terrorism, and so on.

Few are prepared to develop adequate information on these topics through face-to-face contact with informal information sources. The average person is most likely to become informed, gathering whatever information he or she obtains, either directly or indirectly, from the formal sources of mass communication such as newspapers, radio, television, books, magazines, movies, mailings, advertisements, and so on. Thus information, its quality and availability, is directly and intimately connected to the success of the participatory process.

RIGHT TO KNOW

Right to know is argued endlessly.

Journalists call for full access to public information on the grounds that the public has a right to know. Those who argue against such free and open access attribute less altruism to journalists. They claim that the journalist's vested interest (an interest in selling information for commercial gain) is most served by a "right to know." Most commonly heard here is the argument there is some information that the public does not need.

A basis for arguing an extensive public right to know is the suspicion that few people are altruistic enough to be able to ignore their self-interest in making decisions about public needs. That is, the media practitioner does, indeed, disseminate information that "sells," or attracts an audience for commercial advantage. On the other hand, individuals who would restrict distribution of information may be equally as likely to operate from the elitist view that judicious restriction of information tends to reduce social confusion and facilitate the decision-making process for leader groups, among whom they tend to count themselves. The burden of right to know, in short, is placed on individuals and what they "will know" rather than on controllers and what they will distribute.

For what seem to be obvious reasons for a participatory society, the public's "right to know" should, at any point of conflict, be more extensive than limited. If the First Amendment purposely keeps

channels open on the basis of the need for citizens to know and on the
assumption they have the ability to make valid decisions about their
environment, then a right to know is not only a privilege granted by
society, but a compelling necessity.

In either case, the concept of public right to know relies heavily on the
collective judgments of journalists and other mass communicators for
the breath of life.

If that is so, a broad right to know should be of paramount concern to
the journalist who is committed to preserving a pluralistic and
participatory society, and the journalist who fails to be a pluralist
commits an ethical transgression. A public right to know is of little
moment in our evolving world unless the concept of pluralism is implicit
in the structure that gives it life.

Some may argue that "the system" provides for adequate right to
know, with the First Amendment guaranteeing a right to establish
communication channels that will make adequate distribution likely.

However, periodic legal activities and debates have demonstrated
that the First Amendment only makes possible the opening up of
channels. It still requires a moral commitment—not legal actions—to
assure open channels.

Richard Schwarzlose glimpsed, by 1977, a drift toward legal
affirmation of a public right to know characterized by two instances
separated in time. A series of "positive demands" were made on the mass
media to grant the public such a right (specifically, it was a question of
opening the press to public access, a right-to-know concept): the
findings of the 1947 Commission on Freedom of the Press and the early
1970s campaign by Jerome Barron as he argued an implied First
Amendment right of access. Although three decades separate the two
events, emphasizing that the issue refuses to die, the stronger Barron
proposal utimately lost in the courts in the Tornillo case in which the
U.S. Supreme Court refused to affirm a right of access. The Court
reiterated the right of a newspaper's publisher to nearly absolute control
of its content. Thus the scope of coverage is a matter of conscience for
the publisher-journalist. Not law.

Schwarzlose thus saw his suggestion that the courts might be
increasingly inclined to allow a public-oriented right-to-know position,
rather than journalist or media oriented, clearly rejected.

Electronic media have attracted such vast audiences that a
government-mandated access, through the regulating power of the
Federal Communications Commission, could make guaranteed access a

reality. Yet recent debates suggest future deregulation of electronic media, rather than expanded regulation, may yet deny assured access.

Many media-watchers, deploring media tendencies to restrict access by holders of unpopular views, or views that challenge the status quo, tend to look to government intervention to pry open the channels. Yet, right to know, not likely to be fostered by government mandate, is—again—constitutionally a matter of media ethics. Let us assume that the less government intervenes in media matters, the more likely society will maintain dynamism and growth by opening up information flow. That is, look at an "open" communication system as infinitely more desirable to society's well-being and view the "closing" of the system through even a "positive" government act of opening access as sinister and harmful.

Linking "right to know" and "pluralism" as two basic components of a participatory society, it seems obvious that, in order for consistently intelligent social decisions to be made, adequate information to the individual produces greater awareness of alternatives in any decision-making opportunity.

Indeed, a basic definition of freedom involves the availability of alternatives. If there are no alternatives, an individual is not free, no matter how desirable the course before him or her. With alternatives, the individual has freedom in direct relation to the number of alternatives.

If the media must function in this way, with minimum government intervention (even as an intervention mood seems to grow in the United States), the journalist has an implied ethical mandate to strengthen rather than rend the fabric of society; and this can best be accomplished by accepting the ethical imperative to function as a pluralist committed to a right to know—certainly rather than as an advocate and perhaps even as a neutralist.

AN ETHICAL IMPERATIVE

The *ethical imperative* for the press and/or mass media places squarely on that industry the challenge of being largely responsible for making the open society work. The industry, furthermore, is in the remarkable position of making that contribution in an environment almost completely free of regulation.

The First Amendment to the Constitution prohibits Congress from making any law restricting freedom of speech or of the press. The Fourteenth Amendment extends that press protection to state and local jurisdictions.

Many argue that the First Amendment has outlived its usefulness and that some regulation is essential if the media are to be harnessed to the plow of social utility. They suggest that the protection was granted under conditions that no longer exist.

Most Letters to the Editor columns nowadays reflect some considerable discomfort at the thought that the fate of society rests in the hands of a band of undisciplinable rabble who call themselves journalists and, through them, the full population. They would prefer that power in the hands of a few "responsible" folk who have demonstrated their abilities by moving into positions of power and influence.

Yet, as the U.S. Supreme Court repeatedly affirms, the First Amendment is the guide for permissible press controls and, by extension, the directions society will take.

Given that freedom, or the absence of restraint, media practitioners must look to their individual and collective ethics or sense of moral judgment to help them knit, rather than rend, the fabric of society that places so much dependence on uncontrolled information systems.

This makes a basic assumption that the vast majority of practitioners are committed to strengthen with their work. History shows this to be so, though there are spectacular examples to the contrary. Such examples tend to demonstrate the resiliency of society, the ability to adjust to incompetent, venal media people. Controllers tend to assume a brittleness in society that allows little leeway for media freedom. Such rigidity has never been demonstrated.

As journalists examine their ethics, they should recognize that the basic purpose of an ethic is not to protect the strong from the weak, but to protect the defenseless or powerless, to distribute power—a condition in which a participatory society is most likely to function best.

Distribution of information through the media is, in a very real sense, a reallocating of power. If done comprehensively, it reduces power of a few by placing information in the hands of all who are interested, making power monopolies difficult to sustain. Power monopolies are anathema in participatory societies.

The Securities and Exchange Commission (SEC) recognizes the corrupting influences of power concentrations by dealing harshly with those who trade on "insider information" to exploit those without such information.

Examination of social institutions shows broad acceptance of the principle of information distribution. Further, if media accept the ethic of distribution, the republic can prosper. If not, power will, in a remorseless way, accumulate in an ever-narrowing base of people. The First Amendment makes it possible for a people to control their own individual and national destinies in an orderly way, through the open and comprehensive distribution of information.

On these terms, the entire media industry, by and large, must accept the mandate to distribute in order for the society to succeed. This is analogous to a business community that accepts a free marketplace mandate and is reluctant to seek regulation when foreign competition looks formidable. The prospect of "protected" markets is tempting, but the long-term prospects for a society in which there is neither business nor information competition are frightening.

In the same way, a government that requires inclusion of "pluralistic" messages in the media in the name of access also has the long-term capacity to mandate other content, much of which history shows is likely to be self-serving and self-perpetuating.

Perhaps there are few better contemporary examples than the 1983 U.S. invasion of Grenada to illustrate the problem of closing channels through government intervention. In this case, it was in the name of national security.

Reporters were not allowed into Grenada until long after the significant events had taken place. By then, reporters no longer had the ability to determine whether dangers cited by the government were real. Although there was some criticism of the military's actions, Americans had little specific, reliable, pluralistic information on which to judge the merits of the Grenada invasion.

In the aftermath, it is not surprising that the U.S. invasion of Grenada received an 80% approval rating in public opinion polls. Perhaps the invasion was justified, but in the absence of informed and robust—perhaps even vitriolic—debate about the merits of the invasion, a more realistic public assessment of the action is impossible. The pluralism of multiple views is critically important and should be routine, but it must be based on specific and fairly complete information.

The ethical imperative, then, demands that most journalists accept, for the good of the order, a responsibility to keep channels open and to stimulate debate.

PLURALISM

Pluralism is the social structure that allows, and even assures, the distribution of multiple messages, or the identification of alternatives. Its obverse is a monism in which society is dominated by a single value system, a "certain knowledge" of what is right. Such certainty allows almost a casual suppression of dissenting views. This condition grows as a single-value system becomes stronger.

A pluralistic society, on the other hand, finds it necessary to tolerate a wide range of views. That tolerance breeds recognition of the need for broad discussion and an impatience with visceral decision making.

The pluralist is described by Roy Macridis and Robert Ward (1972, p. 13) as "a man [or woman] who belongs to many groups" and is neither a "hero nor a scoundrel." But this person is a moderate who becomes "a tolerant man [or woman]." Open-mindedness results from "knowing his [or her] own interests and loyalties [the pluralist]; understands and tolerates those of others."

The advocate, on the other hand, is characterized as intolerant and close-minded. For most who do not make a conscious effort at pluralism, John Stevens (1974) says, "tolerance is an unnatural state." Single-value systems tend to be almost offhandedly suppressive of minorities.

It is natural for a majority to structure its environment in a way that will be self-serving and self-perpetuating. The more powerful the majority, the more likely it will perpetuate its own values.

Even a brief view of the "quaint" cultures of most developing countries shows the ultimate consequences of this syndrome. Many of those societies decided generations, or even centuries, ago that a nearly perfect state had been reached and that life could not be better—"This is the way it is supposed to be." As a consequence, these cultures shut down the discussion mechanism and became "instructional" (closed) societies bent on perpetuating life the way it was, rather than dynamic societies seeking change and improvement.

It is these freeze-frame cultures of hundreds of years ago that tourists today delight in visiting, but that still resist the new ideas that would reduce infant mortality, improve quality of life, provide the education that leads to individual enrichment, and raise life expectancy by decades. As monism assumes social control, so does the prospect of an "instructional" society replacing a "discussional" society, with the consequent slowing or halting of progress and innovation.

Once a society decides to impose formal mandates on its media systems, it takes the first step toward an instructional culture. Again, remember, it is done in the "good cause" of providing a comfortable environment for the culture—not unlike the cultures of long ago—and for the present.

John Merrill has suggested repeatedly (1974, among others) that the fallacy of a Social Responsibility system of media is that it is in danger of becoming a system of formalized controls. Once the media begin to accept restrictions, he says, they have taken their first steps toward authoritarian, autocratic control. It may well be that the transition would take generations, but it is inevitable.

Pluralism implies a constant tension with monists, not an elimination of the conflict. It is this conflict that sees to the relatively full discussion of topics large and small. It is from such dynamic tension that growth and development occurs.

Pluralism guarantees some social tension (with the consequent, and not inconsiderable, skills for dealing with such tension) and conflict, with the resulting progress. Monism, on the other hand, drives toward an appearance of consensus and reduction of conflict, with a resulting "closing" of the information system that discourages pluralism, and results in loss of conflict-resolving social skills.

Elisabeth Noelle-Neumann (1984) documents in her "spiral of silence" theory that contrary voices tend to be extinguished when people sense that expression of their true view will result in social isolation. Applying her "spiral" theory, it seems clear that pluralism will be discouraged as monism is strengthened. She would, it seems logical, find that pluralism becomes more difficult as people become more accustomed to not listening or contributing to pluralistic activities.

Pluralism, a critical element in a society that expects broad participation among its citizens, determines the range of views circulating in the marketplace of public debate. Simply put, citizens may be restricted to the limited freedom of deciding whether to accept or reject a point of view or the much greater freedom of deciding from several differing views. The difference is a critical one, distinguishing a democracy from an autocracy.

Professional literature contains a number of brief, implicit operational definitions of journalistic pluralism, with most suggesting that the journalist's responsibility is primarily political; as Nick Williams

(1966, p. 174) sees it, "to distribute a full range of information, upon which the electorate, and possibly even the national parties will be able to take action." This obviously looks at pluralism as a responsibility of the individual journalist, suggesting that the journalist must assure that freedom of selection exists in fact as well as in theory.

Press pluralism that extends beyond political bounds as an essential element in the survival of a democratic society has deep roots in the Libertarian ideal. Merrill and Lowenstein (1979, p. 89) see an interdependent relationship and suggest, "We might say that the concept of the newspaper press is that of observer and critic of government, and *protector of pluralism*" (emphasis added).

By its very nature, pluralism does not produce easy definitions. Indeed, Merrill and Lowenstein (1979, p. 88) see that institutionalizing the concept of press pluralism creates a paradox.

Because of the Libertarian nature of the concept, little can be done to formalize pluralism, for the very act of formalization is an act of structuring, an act of regulation that journalists do (and should) resist.

The virtue of informal, unstructured pluralism is that it leads to a free encounter of information and ideas and somehow, out of the battle of contradictions, will emerge Truth. It is this rather mystical expectation of a natural process that Merrill and Lowenstein see as having enthroned pluralism in the press system. Such a formulation often leads to journalists refusing to listen "to reason," or to be "responsible."

Journalists, for example, consistently resist legal judgments ordering them to disclose sources or to turn notes over to the courts in order that a "fair trial" may be guaranteed. Or, they consistently seek to acquire and publish information despite laws protecting that information (the famous Pentagon Papers provide an excellent case in point). Their purpose may well be to publish material that will attract an audience, but it is more than incidental that resistance to regulations and restrictions will keep information channels open. Compliance, on the other hand, leads to closing of channels or a reduction of information in public hands.

Inherent in pluralism, though "responsibility" is desirable and even essential for the functioning of society, are (a) a high degree of subjectivity and (b) resistance to social norms. "Responsible" must remain an individual decision left to the communicator in an unregulated media system.

Difficulty in conceptualizing the notion discourages exploration of pluralism as it contributes in a positive way to the ability of an individual to function in a participatory society. However, pluralism produces a dynamic, progressive society because a pluralistic society taps the creativity and resources of all who would contribute, rather than the selectivity of using only those who conform to social norms.

Meshing the ideas, it is apparent that the basic components of pluralism are alternative viewpoints and an empathic tolerance for fairly considering those alternatives. True pluralists, for example, cannot afford the luxury, or the arrogance, of thinking they are right. They realize few truths are absolute and acknowledge that they must deal with a world where right and wrong are usually wedded to a point of view, and often may be identified only in retrospect.

THE ETHICS OF PLURALISM

The *ethical imperative* to be pluralistic is particularly important when society, in the absence of regulation, must rely on men and women of good will for sustenance. This applies in abstract informational ways as it does in physical terms. The starving or poverty-stricken often must rely on the good will of others to provide them with physical necessities, though there may be no legal imperative requiring those others to make the contributions. In the same way, the First Amendment makes it possible, without a requirement, for an audience and media synergy to see to the adequate distribution of information without interference of either law or custom.

Such an imperative also must assume certain abilities by audience members. Many argue that, as we saw earlier, people cannot be trusted with certain information. Yet, inevitably it must be recognized that the Constitution and the courts repeatedly and recently have certified the population as sane and rational and not needing protection from the print media. Congressional debates are discussing whether audiences can be trusted to respond as rationally to unregulated electronic media.

In that event, and in the same way an impoverished villager in Ethiopia must rely on the good will of others, so must audiences in the United States rely on journalists of good will to provide information needed to function, to make decisions. There is no guarantee an individual will receive that information. Quite the contrary. That information is subject to the whims of an informational system that pummels, punches, reshapes, and suppresses information according to predispositions of gatekeepers.

Ethically, then, there is the need for voluntary recognition and acceptance of the responsibility to provide information that will not rip the social fabric. This obviously is a matter of individual definition, but it is that type of discretion that the First Amendment encourages in the expectation that good will decisions will by far outweigh the venal and self-serving determinations by practitioners that are socially destructive.

It may even be that the ethical imperative is helped along by the free marketplace idea that if the information is of sufficient value, it will attract the type of audience that makes it commercially marketable.

There is a different, system-oriented approach maintaining that pluralism among mass media units is the basis of pluralistic responsibility. The staple argument is that general publications will provide pluralistic messages and a variety of special interest publications provide, cumulatively, pluralistic variety.

E. B. White (1976, pp. 52-54) capsulizes the notion as "the privilege of each individual in our society to have access to hundreds of periodicals, each peddling its belief. There is safety in numbers; papers expose each other's follies . . . and cancel out each other's biases."

Such differences in emphasis may be critical; in a very practical way, they determine whether the individual reader will be exposed to pluralistic materials.

An internal resolve, within both the reporter and the media unit, may guarantee the pluralism of a single newspaper or television station. But White's example of multiunit pluralism may not, in this day and age, be sufficient to assure a pluralism of ideas for the individual reader or viewer.

It is clear, as the electronic revolution progresses, that audiences are dividing themselves into smaller, more specialized units. For example, in 1955 most metropolitan newspapers, with their morning or evening competition, could count on reaching nearly 100% of households in the market area. By 1985, that combined percentage was often as low as 50%. As audiences move, they distribute themselves across a range of sources. Few television news programs enjoy more than a 25% share of a given market, leaving the remaining 75% distributed across multiple channels (over-the-air, cable, direct broadcast satellite, and so on).

These and other audience habit patterns make it clear that audiences are increasingly tailoring their consumption habits to personal tastes. No longer can media systems described by E. B. White count on two units achieving saturation in a market.

With the spread of audiences across many units, the interunit pluralism White describes is increasingly impractical for two related reasons:

(1) The same characteristics that cause monistic cultures to protect themselves from tension and conflict appear in individuals. People cannot benefit from pluralism if they isolate themselves from alternative messages. Thus individuals tend to seek reinforcing messages rather than court conflict. They "settle" the matter in their own minds, eliminating the need for further exploration. Once their minds are made up, and if conditions permit, they are likely to conveniently avoid information that will disturb the decision.

(2) As the proliferating media industry becomes more and more competitive, a willingness grows among writers and editors to provide audiences with what they want rather than with what, perhaps, is important or necessary. An extreme example might be seen in the special interest publications that attract readers with a specific predisposition. It is highly unlikely, for example, that the official magazine of the National Rifle Association (NRA), as it strives to assure the rights of gun enthusiasts, will balance its coverage with vigorous gun-control articles. Thus, as audiences increasingly have the ability to control the information they receive (with principles of item 1, above, at work) it is increasingly possible for strong gun enthusiasts to arrange their information intake in such a way that they would be able to avoid almost completely any of the pluralistic discussions surrounding the gun control controversy. They would be able to assure that all their information support their views, therefore solidifying their attitudes. Emergence of such a system of information could very well sound the death knell of public discussion in the United States, endangering the very element of discussion the First Amendment is presumably designed to encourage.

This growing ability to control information intake almost completely by limiting sources suggests a strong need for intraunit pluralism in order for the intelligent decision to be possible. That is, in the extreme, there may come a time that the NRA should accept a responsibility to balance gun-control arguments. Failure to do this would accelerate development of a polarized society, hardened attitudes, and the strong probability of a reversion to violence in solution to social problems.

Alvin Toffler, in both *Future Shock* (1970) and *The Third Wave* (1981), and John Naisbitt, in *Megatrends* (1982), see increasing individuality, a tailoring of the individuals' own media to their interests, with the consequent tailoring of the views they encounter.

Toffler suggests that this headlong rush in search of variety, choice, and freedom is leading to a social fragmentation that is bringing about "the crackup of consensus."

Don Pember (1974) also notes accelerating disintegration of the mass audience, noting the ongoing demise of general interest publications and the meteoric growth of publications—and other media—aimed at smaller, specialized target publics. He says that social fragmentation shows no signs of slowing down and predicts that "this fact alone portends great problems for the mass media in America." He believes the day is rapidly coming when everything a person gets from the media can be stored in a computer and called up on a tailor-made basis. "On that day, mass media no longer exist," says Pember (1974, pp. 331-359).

When mass media cease to exist, the good will of people in discussing issues through interpersonal media becomes critical.

Fisher (1972, p. 13) shares the vision and finds it ironic that "the technology that threatens to end individuality bears within itself the seeds of diversity as well. It is possible that the mass media . . . may someday be replaced by a host of special media, each serving its special audiences and their special interest."

Given that kind of situation, it is not difficult to envision an age of specialization of such magnitude that each source will become an advocate or special pleader delivering its messages to its special publics without the benefit of pluralized alternatives that provide for public dialogue and consensual decision making.

People cannot benefit from pluralism if they are isolated from alternative messages by the velvety cocoon of special interest and come into contact only with advocate-type messages.

Therefore, in the absence of legislation, ethics must emerge as the driving force in serving the republic. This suggests that people of good will are expected to emerge and voluntarily accept the responsibility, without a mandate of law, to provide the information that will allow society to function and flourish. In order for them to emerge, they must recognize the importance of the contribution they are asked to make, and they must be able to realistically recognize the formidable barriers they face in filling that responsibility.

The mass communicator with a commitment to pluralism must fight two forces: (1) forces that would gain control of messages by consolidation of power and (2) countervailing forces that threaten to stratify and specialize messages. Both serve to limit the number of voices, and—by corollary—pluralistic ideas the reader or viewer will encounter.

This problem is compounded by the fact that the journalist is also caught in a tug-of-war between those who would control information in order to influence public decisions and those who must make the decisions but feel threatened when alternative views emerge that tend to challenge their own opinions.

The pluralist-journalists find themselves in the vortex of a maelstrom that would prevent them from identifying alternatives and presenting them to their audience. It is a position requiring dedication, perseverance, hard work, and a toughness of mind that will not permit them to take the relatively easy course of advocate.

Their position is one that will be unpopular, unappreciated and unrewarding. Nevertheless, it is a role necessary to the perpetuation of a free society where participatory democracy relies on the alternative information they provide.

Despite the lip service paid to pluralism, much of it indirect, in the communication industry, it is a difficult standard by which to live. Therefore, it would seem that pluralism must be encouraged and emphasized as a positive virtue if it is to survive the stresses of contemporary communication trends.

A dedicated pluralist is one who almost automatically thinks of and introduces at least a second side of an issue into both professional stories and private conversations.

Under the pluralist mandate, the journalist must become a healthy skeptic who assumes that when a source makes a statement, one or more alternative positions should be publicly examined before decisions are reached.

Merrill and Lowenstein (1979, p. 147) call the pluralistic position a criterion "that might help the student of the press evaluate a newspaper."

How well, they ask, does the newspaper achieve a diversity of news and views? Is there an attempt to provide some kind of balance or argument in the opinion columns and a realistic range of viewpoints and subject matter in the news columns?

These questions are at the root of the pluralistic ethic.

Perhaps to counter pernicious effects of both external pressures and individual biases, it would be fruitful to teach the spirit and rationale of the "scientific method" to journalists. This spirit, described by philosopher C. S. Peirce, "requires a man to be at all times ready to dump his whole cartload of beliefs the moment experience is against them. The desire to learn forbids him to be perfectly cocksure that he knows already" (Lee, 1941, p. 70).

Such an attitude by journalists tends to immunize them from the inevitable persuasive rhetoric of the special pleader and instills in them a critical sense that "this is not *all* the story".

But this state is more easily discussed than achieved: Consider the fact that, of a corps of hundreds of highly experienced Washington correspondents, only two were convinced to the point of action that the government had not been telling the true story about Watergate-related events. Yet tales circulating through professional circles at the time suggested a far wider recognition of corruption surrounding the Nixon Administration and the Watergate adventure. It is far easier to be an advocate, for it is a path of least resistance. Tolerance is often a painful state, and a commitment to pluralism requires a journalist to distribute views that may be personally repugnant.

Advocates will at least receive the accolades of their ideological bedfellows. Pluralists have little such social refinement. Their commitment requires them to reconcile themselves to harsh treatment by the special pleaders on all sides and generally ignored by the public they try to provide with alternative information. The Grenada invasion is an excellent recent example. Some 80% of the American people supported the invasion, leaving little doubt that journalists would not be thanked for pressing vigorously for information alternative to that released by the government.

It is a thankless task at best because the pluralist is committed to long-range objectives rooted in the freedom ethic whereas, as Stevens (1974, p. 23) notes, "Both men and societies usually opt for short-term goals."

Pluralism traditionally is in short supply, even among the media. As Stevens (1974, p. 23) points out,

> American publishers have always been willing to allow suppression of the radical press; often they have led the efforts to punish. Many local papers in 1969 were urging and applauding convictions of college and underground editors for printing "dirty words." The general press seldom has been willing to align itself with those elements whose views are unpopular.

Compounding the problem is the constant accusatory pressure by "in" powers that the media are ideologically opposed to current public opinion—a natural condition, but one that ideologues exploit.

John Milton (1937, p. 189) viewed as "the utmost bound of civil liberty attained" a situation in which "complaints are freely heard, deeply considered, and speedily reformed."

Therefore, it is entirely appropriate that the media should publish complaints of the "in" powers against them. However, the problem emerges when the media lose the will to continue distribution of pluralistic views.

In the absence of legal restraints in the United States, there is a resort to strategies to control the media. Complaints by the administration and others are, and have been for generations, among strategies used to manipulate the media. No in-power group is excited about media pluralism. The in-group tends to have access to the media by virtue of its power position, and pluralism is seen as a way of reducing the power of that group. Therefore, that group uses the media to cause the media, if they will, to ignore their own responsibilities.

Milton (1937, p. 22) takes an optimistic view of audiences, suggesting in his opposition to the licensing of printing in England that leaders and media ought

consider what nation it is whereof ye are, and whereof ye are the governors: a nation not slow and dull, but of a quick, ingenious and piercing spirit, accute to invent, subtle and sinewy to discourse, not beneath the reach of any point the highest that human capacity can soar to.

Such an optimistic view of the populace would seem to be a basic premise the Bill of Rights imposes on this nation about the nature of its inhabitants. Therefore, under terms laid down by the First Amendment, it would seem reasonable that a journalist in this society must be committed to at least the first element of Milton's "utmost bound of civil liberty attained." The first element suggests an ethical imperative resting on the journalist to strive to guarantee that "complaints are freely heard" in the broadest sense of the word. Indeed, to exercise regulation of information (by the journalist) either by sins of omission (ignoring certain viewpoints) or by sins of commission (engaging in unilateral persuasion), journalists are either insulting their audience (or showing some considerable contempt) or are arrogantly deciding what course is best in a given matter and denying that audience the right to make the decision. The first is intolerable in a participatory society and the second may ultimately institutionalize a mistaking of vested interest for the social interest.

All mandates must have a source from which they derive their power and authority. The source of the pluralist mandate (or the ethical imperative) is the ethic of freedom—an ethic upon which this nation has reached consensual agreement and that operates on the premise that a person has the right (and the ability) to make personal choices from among a body of well-articulated alternatives.

Failure to provide the alternatives amounts to an ethical violation— but it is a violation that cannot be regulated or punished because members of a free society must be free to either uphold the freedom ethic or abrogate their responsibilities.

Herein lies the dilemma of the advocate journalist, or of the special pleader.

Advocacy is a seductive concept for journalists because it allows them to justify their actions as steps to reform. Caught up in a messianic zeal, or even submerged in a subtle bias (professional or personal), they fail to provide alternative information because they are somehow convinced that their advocacy will be the salvation of society or satisfy another noble purpose. But in a very real sense, advocates renege on their responsibility by using the medium they control to become special pleaders and thereby skewing—if not upsetting—the informational balance of power so vital to a participatory society.

Indeed, it seems clear that the journalist who does not adopt a pluralist ethic becomes an advocate either by choice or by default. Whether a person fails to present alternatives by free choice or professional sloth, the end result is the same.

SUMMARY

To summarize, conditions of press consolidation and the emergence of more specialized media and audiences have made most assumptions relative to press pluralism obsolete while at the same time sharpening the need for examination of the topic.

These assumptions generally held that the more publications and public voices there are, the more sources of information (in terms of media units), the more pluralism was served.

Specialized audiences and a tendency of audiences to bring themselves into contact mostly with supporting, reinforcing points of view have raised the question of whether individual journalists might need to consider the urgency of an ethical mandate that they become pluralists and for the ethic of pluralism to shift from intermedia to intramedia in its nature.

A difficult responsibility is to generate and present messages presenting alternatives to those of organized, special pleading individuals.

Such generation of alternative messages allows individual audience members in a participatory society to consider options in their decision-making processes. In a nation committed to ultimate governance by public opinion, the pluralistic journalist becomes an essential element in the production by society of decisions that, in the light of history, will be correct.

That the public has the continuing capacity for making correct decisions is a basic premise of the legal structure built around the First and Fourteenth Amendments. At question is the continuing possibility for making those decisions. Continuing and expanding societal problems are predicted unless journalists accept an ethical mandate to provide each audience with alternatives or options for the decisions the audience members must make.

The alternative is sharp polarization and resort to violence, rather than discussion, in resolving social confrontations.

REFERENCES

Fisher, R. M. (1972, September). The challenging role of the newsman. *Neiman Reports*, *XXVI*(3).
Lee, I. J. (1941). *Language habits in human affairs*. New York: Harper & Row.
Macridis, R. C., & Ward, R. E. (1972). *Modern political systems: Europe*. Englewood Cliffs, NJ: Prentice-Hall.
Merrill, J. C. (1974). *The imperative of freedom*. New York: Hastings House.
Merrill, J., & Lowenstein, R. L. (1979). *Media, messages and man* (2nd Ed.). New York: Longman.
Milton, J. (1937). Aeropagitica, In C. W. Eliot (Ed.), *The Harvard classics: Bacon, Milton, Brown volume*. New York: P. F. Collier & Sons.
Naisbitt, J. (1982). *Megatrends: Ten new directions transforming our lives*. New York: Warner.

Noelle-Neumann, E. (1984). *The spiral of silence: Public opinion, our social skin.* Chicago: University of Chicago Press.

Pember, D. (1974). *Mass media in America.* Chicago: Science Research Associates.

Schwarzlose, R. (1977, July/August). For journalists only. *Columbia Journalism Review.*

Stevens, J. D. (1974). Freedom of expression: A new dimension. In H. Clor (Ed.), *Mass and modern democracy.* Chicago: Rand-McNally.

Toffler, A. (1970). *Future Shock.* New York: Bantam.

Toffler, A. (1981). *The third wave.* New York: Bantam.

What E. B. White told Xerox (1976, September/October). In *Columbia Journalism Review,* September-October.

Williams, N. B. (1966). America's third force: The watchdog press. In G. Gross (Ed.), *The responsibility of the press.* New York: Fleet.

5

PRESS RESPONSIBILITY AND
FIRST AMENDMENT VALUES

Theodore L. Glasser

It is an old and familiar argument that a truly free press is a press free to disregard its duty to be responsible. Many have expressed this point of view, but none more bluntly than the distinguished journalist Vermont Royster (n.d.): "There can be no freedom of the press unless the press has the right to be irresponsible."

Notwithstanding the importance of a responsible press, Royster believes that "responsibility must lie in the conscience of each of us"; and because, in Royster's view, an individual's conscience should not be the basis for determining an individual's liberty, "The editor who is without conscience must be free—if it comes to that—to be irresponsible." Thus for Royster and others whose views reflect an essentially libertarian construction of the First Amendment, questions of responsibility are effectively reduced to questions of conscience; and because questions of conscience are rendered utterly irrelevant to the ideal of a free press, there can be no necessary connection between freedom of the press and press responsibility.

Royster's conception of a free press captures rather well what I think can be fairly termed the dominant interpretation of the First Amendment—dominant particularly among contemporary American journalists. To be sure, it is the dominant interpretation among those who view freedom of the press from a Lockean natural-rights perspective; among those who believe that only a "minimal state," to use Robert Nozick's (1974) term, can protect and preserve individual liberty; among those who regard any form of press regulation—no matter how benign—as constitutionally impermissible; and among those who summarily reject all models of press accountability save the "marketplace," which is acceptable only because it is taken to be self-evidently natural. It is, at bottom, the dominant interpretation of the First Amendment among those whose moral philosophy focuses on individual self-interest, a tradition in ethics known as "egoism."

My goal here is to argue against the libertarian construction of the First Amendment and to offer in its place an interpretation that will fully accommodate what has for too long been the largely irreconcilable ideals of a free and responsible press. Specifically, my objectives are four: (1) to review the power and appeal of the libertarian view of press freedom, with emphasis on its most enduring metaphor—the "marketplace of ideas"; (2) to examine the consequences of a press wedded to a marketplace model of press accountability; (3) to sketch the contours of an alternative view of the meaning of freedom of the press, an interpretation grounded in what has been called "positive" or "affirmative" theories of the First Amendment; and (4) to assess the implications of this alternative view for journalists and the larger community journalists seek to serve.

LIBERTARIANISM AND THE
ROMANCE OF THE MARKETPLACE

Libertarianism begins and ends with the preeminence of individual liberty. It embraces liberty as the ultimate political value, a fundamentally natural and thus inalienable right of the individual to deny claims of obligation or authority. Intellectually indebted to John Locke and Adam Smith, today's libertarian can cite with approval a variety of contemporary thinkers, including novelist-philosopher Ayn Rand and economists Friedrich Hayek, Ludwig Von Mises, and Milton Friedman; and since 1974, libertarians have had at their disposal Robert Nozick's *Anarchy, State, and Utopia*, which almost single-handedly reawakened interest in—and brought a degree of respectability to—the study of libertarian ideas, particularly as those ideas might be studied by academic philosophers (see Machan, 1982).

Nozick's treatise, which he would like to read as a philosophical exploration and not as a political tract, is in many ways an elaborate theory of entitlement—an extended argument about what people are entitled to have and what people are entitled to do with what they have.

Following the "respectable tradition of Locke," Nozick (1974, p. 10) posits a system of liberty managed principally by the forces of nature; for individuals subject only to the "laws of nature," Locke reminds us, are in "a state of perfect freedom to order their actions and dispose of their possessions and persons as they think fit." Accordingly, Nozick favors a narrowly defined role for the state, a basically "night-watchman" role limited "to the function of protecting all its citizens against violence, theft, and fraud, and to the enforcement of contracts, and so on" (p. 26). This is what Nozick means by the "minimal state," which he presents as the "morally favored state, the only morally legitimate state, the only morally tolerable one"; any more extensive state, Nozick argues, could only inhibit our freedom "to choose our life and to realize our ends and our conception of ourselves, insofar as we can, aided by the voluntary cooperation of other individuals" (pp. 333-334).

The minimal state—presumably the only state to treat its citizens as "inviolate individuals"—constitutes Nozick's "framework for utopia." Although not utopia itself, the minimal state—and only the minimal state—fosters a utopian process, which is as far as Nozick needs to go; for utopia, as Nozick envisions it, is whatever "grows spontaneously from the individual choices of many people over a long period of time" (p. 332).

Thus Nozick and his fellow libertarians share an aversion to what Tibor Machan (1983) calls the "petty tyranny of government regulation," the often popular but nonetheless "immoral" effort by the state to move beyond merely protecting and preserving individual liberty. In principle, it is an aversion to the state accepting responsibility for the "general welfare" of its citizens: mandating education, ensuring access to health care, providing safe products, redistributing wealth, establishing standards of employment, and other similarly altruistic policies that, in the end, only diminish individuals by treating them as "morally impotent, wards of the state, dependents, or fundamentally incapacitated by their circumstances to prepare for what is after all, a life with risks, small and great" (Machan, 1983, p. 287). In practice, however, the libertarian's aversion to the tyranny of government regulation often manifests itself in narrower terms: opposition to the state's economic directives and the "legal coercion" used to enforce them.

Because economic freedom looms large in the libertarian's sense of social and political justice, the metaphor of the marketplace has had wide and lasting appeal. For more than three centuries, in fact, the marketplace metaphor has been called into service to combat one of the state's most perilous policies: suppression of expression.

John Milton's *Areopagitica*, his eloquent plea in 1644 for the liberty of unlicensed printing, essentially called for open competition among ideas. Let truth and falsehood grapple, Milton said; "who ever knew Truth put to the worse, in a free and open encounter?" (pp. 35-36). Thomas Jefferson used a similar theme when he wrote the 1785 preamble to the Virginia Statute of Religious Freedom, which portrayed truth as the "proper and sufficient antagonist to error"; truth "has nothing to fear from the conflict," Jefferson wrote, "unless by human interposition disarmed of her natural weapons" (quoted in Emerson, 1977, p. 740). And Oliver Wendell Holmes, in one of the Supreme Court's most remembered dissenting opinions, observed,

> When men have realized that time has upset many fighting faiths, they may come to believe even more than they believe the very foundations of their own conduct that the ultimate good desired is better reached by free trade in ideas—that the best test of truth is the power of the thought to get itself accepted in the competition of the market, and that truth is the only ground upon which their wishes safely can be carried out. (*Abrams v. U.S.*, 250 U.S. 616, 630 [1919])

These and other allusions to the power of competition and the value of free trade underscore the libertarian's abiding faith in the principle of laissez-faire; and, historically, they vivify the libertarian's enduring confidence in the relationship between economic freedom and freedom of expression (see Smith, 1981; Owen, 1975). The marketplace metaphor, therefore, represents nothing less—and, significantly, nothing more—than an unqualified commitment to individual autonomy and freedom of choice.

In their application to journalism, it follows, the tenets of libertarianism translate into a "philosophy of journalistic autonomy," which is, appropriately enough, the subtitle of John Merrill's (1974) *The Imperative of Freedom*. A far-ranging disquisition on the virtues of a libertarian view of press freedom, Merrill's impassioned plea for "editoral self-determinism" stands in opposition to what he sees as a dangerous retreat from the very individualism on which rests a truly free press: self-respect, self-realization, self-expression, and self-interest. Specifically, Merrill rails against the institutionalization and professionalization of journalism, which can only lead to conformity and homogeneity; and he laments the growing "suspicion of autonomy" and the resulting "depreciation of libertarianism," which can only undermine the journalist's dignity and sense of independence. Merrill is particularly unhappy with "fuzzy social utilitarian thinking" about the press, which has its roots in the "elitist" Hutchins Commission and its 1947 report on *A Free and Responsible Press*. Merrill (1974, p. 204), indeed, finds the current preoccupation with the "nascent concept of 'social responsibility'" to be a real and substantial threat to press freedom:

> The concept of "social responsibility," however good it may sound, is one which the libertarian journalist should approach with great care. The current emphasis on "social responsibility in journalism may well be nothing more than a subterfuge under which elite groups or persons go about trying to make the press system over in their own image. Self-realization demands a rejection of the whole concept of social responsibility—except that sense in which it might be taken to mean that *personal* responsibility which a free and rational journalist determines for himself. The existential responsibility to one's self and for one's own actions is the responsibility of a free person and a free society.

True to the libertarian ideal that individuals ought to be free to deny claims of obligation or authority, Merrill would prefer no oversight, no accountability—only freedom from government intervention of any sort. For freedom, as Merrill defines it, "implies *freedom not* to accept any obligation or particular responsibility. Obligations and responsibilities are contradictory to freedom, for they limit freedom or restrict it and therefore should be anathema to libertarians" (p. 80).

Thus for Merrill, logically, morality exists only on the level of the individual. Whereas "law is something that is socially determined and socially enforced," ethics, in Merrill's view, is "personally determined and personally enforced." Ultimately, what is right, like what is true, will make itself known through the "self-correcting process" of the marketplace, a process of "proven" value: "In spite of many criticisms which can be hurled at a free and autonomous press for avowed 'errors' and 'excesses' and the like, it is probably safe to say that in the United States, for example, the people are very well informed about the issues of the day, the activities of their elected representatives, and the strengths and weaknesses of their political (and other) institutions" (Merrill, 1974, pp. 164-165).

THE PRIVATIZATION OF PRESS FREEDOM

The metaphor of the marketplace celebrates the importance of the distinction between an individual's "private" and "public" life, a distinction of considerable constitutional consequence. With few exceptions, freedom of the press and other constitutional guarantees apply only to conduct in the public sphere; they apply, that is, only to individuals whose conduct might be subject to what the judiciary calls "state action." A free press, therefore, ordinarily means a press free from public control—a press sufficiently insulated from the specter of state action.

Historically, the First Amendment generally has not been interpreted as a safeguard against control in and by the private sector. Although now and then the state will impose limits on the press, these limits are typically reconciled with—not justified by—constitutional freedoms. When, for example, the Supreme Court ruled in 1937 that Morris Watson, an editorial writer for the Associated Press, could not be fired for engaging in union activity, it was not a decision based on (or justified by) the AP's violation of Watson's freedom of speech or freedom of association. Rather, in a decision that remains "the fountainhead of any understanding of the relationship of labor law to the press" (Gillmor & Barron, 1984, p. 642), the Court found that the National Labor Relations Act, which established employees' collective bargaining rights, did not violate the AP's First Amendment right "to publish the news as it desires it published and to enforce policies of its own choosing with respect to the editing and rewriting of news for publication" (*Associated Press v. National Labor Relations Board*, 301 U.S. 103 [1937]).

Except for the most egregious transgressions (e.g., blatant antitrust violations) or conduct grossly inimical to conventional morality (e.g., obscenity), the actions of the press—particularly when those actions bear on the content of expression—are as a rule subject only to the realities of free enterprise. Generally, in fact, the American version of freedom of the press is little more than a call for the state to recognize the sovereignty of private transactions, which is in effect a recognition of the value of an unregulated marketplace—metaphorically and quite literally. And because this view of press freedom is so deeply imbedded in the American psyche, any contrary position, as supporters of broadcast regulation have learned, is likely to be attacked as a "highly inefficient, illiberal one, quite contrary to the nation's traditions" (Pool, 1983, p. 146).

The traditional and dominant "sovereignty of private transactions" interpretation of the First Amendment prospers not only because it exudes a certain charm, especially in contrast to any authoritarian or totalitarian alternative, but because it subtlely diverts attention from its invariably circumscribed conception of freedom and independence. For although the print and electronic press may wave the banner of freedom and independence, the fact remains that "twenty corporations control more than half the 61 million daily newspapers sold everyday; twenty corporations control more than half the revenues of the country's 11,000 magazines; three corporations control most of the revenues and audience in television; ten corporations in radio; eleven corporations in all kinds of books; and four corporations in motion pictures" (Bagdikian, 1983, p. 4). It is nothing less than Orwellian when publishers and broadcasters preach freedom *of* the press, because in Washington and elsewhere their industry representatives continue to lobby for a more limited and principally proprietary freedom *for* the press.

Decidedly, the politically and thus judicially legitimate view of freedom of expression, which David Kairys (1982, p. 163) properly describes as the prevailing "ideology"[1] of free speech, effectively confines freedom and democracy to the public sphere, where, arguably, expression can flourish with little or no control or suppression. But in the private sector, Kairys points out, "which encompasses almost all economic activity," including the private transactions of the press, "we allow no democracy or equality and only the freedom to buy or sell." In its everyday application, therefore, the prevailing interpretation of the First Amendment inevitably results in a powerful dichotomy between freedom of speech and freedom of the press.

Although the courts offer little guidance in this area, it seems reasonably prudent to define the First Amendment's speech clause as "a protection of the liberty to express ideas and beliefs, while the press clause focuses specifically on the liberty to disseminate expression broadly" (Gillmor & Barron, 1984, p. 154). In theory, perhaps, the difference does not amount to much. In practice, however, the difference is painfully obvious to two large and largely overlapping classes of citizen: those whose financial resources limit their opportunity to disseminate their expressions and those whose expressions find little or no acceptance among the managers of the established media of communications. Thus from the perspective of an increasingly substantial proportion of the citizenry, there exists a widening gap between speech rights and press rights, such that for many citizens the only opportunity for public expression comes in the form of what Kairys calls "displays of displeasure": picketing, demonstrating, distributing leaflets. The larger and often more effective forums for public expression, which include the traditional and thus the more "respectable" print and broadcast media, are readily accessible only to individuals with considerable wealth, power, or status. Kairys (1982, p. 166), then, hardly overstates his case when he concludes that "the ordinary person or group of ordinary persons has no means, based in the Constitution or elsewhere, to engage meaningfully in that dialogue on the issues of the day that the First Amendment is so often heralded as promoting and guaranteeing."

Because the Constitution protects freedom in but not freedom from the private sector, the First Amendment has had little to say about who owns and controls the means of communication. Consequently, the only means of communication truly guaranteed—as opposed to merely protected—are the ones that fall outside the marketplace, and these are characteristically marginal in their ability to reach any but a small and contiguous public. Within the marketplace, as the owners of the press well know, the means of communication are treated as private property and the right of self-expression has become, as Walter Lippmann (1955) once feared, more a private amenity than a public necessity.

As an essentially marketplace construct cloaked in the language of the Constitution, a "free press" denotes an institutional privilege, not an individual right. The internal hierarchy of the marketplace accommodates "freedom" only as a *derivative* right—a liberty derived from owners and extended to subordinates commensurate with the latter's ability and willingness to serve the former's needs and interests.[2] Although the judiciary is understandably reluctant to endorse such a manifestly undemocratic application of a basic constitutional right, its uncompromising faith in the marketplace leaves little opportunity to assess seriously, let alone reject, the inevitable consequences of a press dominated by a handful of entrepreneurs. Thus largely through inaction and indifference the courts move closer and closer to Justice Potter Stewart's position, outlined in a speech at Yale in 1974, which holds that the press clause ought to be read as a structural provision designed to protect the "private business" of the press:

Most of the other provisions in the Bill of Rights protect specific liberties or specific rights of individuals: freedom of speech, freedom of worship, the right to counsel, the privilege against compulsory self-incrimination, to name a few. In contrast, the Free Press Clause extends protection to an institution. The publishing business is, in short, the only organized private business that is given explicit constitutional protection. (Stewart, 1975, p. 633)

AFFIRMATIVE THEORIES OF THE FIRST AMENDMENT

Grounded in the natural rights tradition, marketplace advocates rely on a Darwinian or "survival" theory to defend freedom of choice and individual autonomy. Just as Nozick cannot say what his utopia will look like, except that it will be the result of "the individual choices of many people over a long period of time," libertarians cannot say what the "invisible hand" of the marketplace will bring, except that whatever it brings is presumptively better than what it does not bring. Libertarians, in other words, seldom offer any objective criteria for what the marketplace should produce; rather, "what ought to be" is invariably defined in terms of "what is"—what does survive is what ought to survive.

Frederick Schauer (1982), among others, raises two important objections to the proposition that the marketplace is the best means to some unknown end. First, when applied to questions of truth or quality, marketplace advocates must resort to the most extreme subjectivism, a "majority rule" logic altogether contrary to the notions of value and quality embodied in our language of evaluation; it "distorts out of all recognition our use of words like 'true', 'good', 'sound', or 'wise'" (p. 22). Second, the proposition treats time as inconsequential. Nozick, for instance, has no sense of how long his "framework for utopia" would need to be in place before utopia finally arrives; he knows only that it would be a "long period of time." Similarly, who can say how long it would take before truth or knowledge becomes "self-evident"; who can say, that is, how much "free trade in ideas" is necessary before the "best" ideas emerge? Schauer (1982, p. 27) writes, "If there is no limit to its duration the assertion that knowledge advances in the long run is both irrefutable and meaningless. Yet if the relevant time period is discrete and observable, history furnishes far too many counter-examples for us to have much confidence in the power of truth consistently to prevail."

To reject the marketplace and its metaphor is thus to reject the proposition that freedom should be defined solely as a means to some unspecified end. It is to reject a strictly "negative" or "freedom from" view of liberty. It is to reject the "night-watchman" role as the only role the state can play in preserving and protecting an individual's freedom. And to reject the marketplace and its metaphor is to reject a reading of the First Amendment that interprets "freedom of the press" as merely the freedom to compete.

A "positive" or "affirmative" theory of the First Amendment rejects the traditional dyadic view of liberty: "X is free from Y," where Y represents the obligation or authority from which X, the individual, is free. Instead, an affirmative construction of the First Amendment views liberty as a triadic relation: "X is free from Y to do Z," where Z represents the goal or objective of the relationship between X and Y.[3] Whereas a negative conception of liberty would define freedom of the press as freedom from state interference, a positive conception of liberty would define freedom of the press as freedom from state interference to, say, accommodate and disseminate a broad range of expression. Although the positive view of liberty encompasses the negative view, the difference is crucial: "rights to freedom are rights to the enablements to be free and not only rights to freedom from interference"(Held, 1984, p. 128).

There have been several scholarly treatments of the benefits of an affirmative or positive interpretation of the free press clause, including Zechariah Chafee's pioneering study of *Government and Mass Communications*, which appeared in 1947 as two of several volumes sponsored and published by the Commission on Freedom of the Press (Hutchins Commission); Jerome Barron's (1967; 1969; 1973) proposals for access rights; and Thomas Emerson's (1970; 1981) continuing effort to identify and develop the principles and rules, as he recently expressed it, "for employing governmental powers to expand the system of freedom of expression, while at the same time controlling and limiting those powers" (1981, p. 796).

Chafee, Barron, and Emerson offer broadly similar justifications for enlarging the opportunity for expression. In Chafee's (1947) view, the "mere absence of governmental restrictions will not make newspapers and other instrumentalities of communication play their proper part in the kind of society we desire" (p. 471); the state, therefore, can properly "lay down rules of the game which will promote rather than restrict free speech"(p. 475). Barron (1967), too, recognizes the limits of a "minimal state" approach to the First Amendment, an approach altogether indifferent to the needs of society's disadvantaged and dissatisfied to discuss their grievances openly and effectively. That the conventional understanding of the First Amendment fails to equate liberty with opportunity is, for Barron (1967, p. 1641), an alarming anomaly in our constitutional law:

> While we protect expression once it has come to fore, our law is indifferent to creating opportunities for expression. Our constitutional theory is in the grip of a romantic conception of free expression, a belief that the "marketplace of ideas" is freely accessible. But if ever there were a self-operating marketplace of ideas, it has long ceased to exist. The mass media's development of an antipathy to ideas requires legal intervention if novel and unpopular ideas are to be assured a forum—unorthodox points of view which have no claim on broadcast time and newspaper space as a matter of right are in poor position to compete with those ideas aired as a matter of grace.

And Emerson (1981), whose recent essay on the "affirmative side" of the First Amendment rests squarely on his larger theory of freedom of expression, finds "grave distortions" in the current system of freedom of expression, distortions that "cannot be eased or eliminated without measures that go beyond the traditional safeguards to protect expression against governmental interference, as crucial as those safeguards continue to be" (p. 848).

Fully aware of the danger inherent in a positive view of freedom, especially the risk that the state might exceed its limited jurisdiction, Chafee, Barron, and Emerson nonetheless find major deficiencies in the traditional laissez-faire system that warrant the use of governmental powers to "make available the opportunity for expression as well as protect it from encroachment" (Emerson, 1970, p. 629). To facilitate, promote, or enlarge the opportunities for communication without simultaneously limiting or restricting communication is "emerging as one of the crucial problems of the future," a problem Emerson seeks to resolve by distinguishing between appropriate and inappropriate levels of state intervention.

The state may properly support communication by intervening in a "general area" or a "broad subject-matter" but may not control communication within the area of its intervention. Conceptually, the distinction is one between macro-intervention and micro-intervention, a distinction Emerson (1981, p. 803) likens to the structure of a university: "The administration makes broad decisions with respect to the courses that shall be taught and their basic subject matter, but the individual faculty member is free to control the presentation in a particular classroom." Special safeguards, Emerson acknowledges, may be necessary to ensure that control of the macro area cannot be manipulated to affect control of the micro area.

Chafee employs a similar analogy when he calls attention to the need for newspapers and other "great instrumentalities of communication" to develop their own internal ideals. This can be accomplished, Chafee believes, only when the press is responsive to—and yet ultimately free from—public and private pressure, in much the same way a sufficiently endowed university accepts advice and support from outsiders but in the end lives its own life. A great press and a great university, Chafee argues, should at least have in common their relation to outside forces: Outsiders are welcome to facilitate achievement but never with the power to compel content.

Chafee, Barron, and Emerson approach the topic of an affirmative theory of the First Amendment from different perspectives, and to a degree arrive at different conclusions, but they agree in principle that the goal of a free press is something more than a free press. Without denying the value of viewing freedom as an end in itself, they recognize that freedom often serves other goals, and that these other goals may become part of the justification for preserving and protecting freedom. Such is the case with freedom of the press, a freedom defined—and defended— not only in terms of the press itself but in terms of the larger society as well. In the final analysis, the work of Chafee, Barron, and Emerson invites the press to acknowledge that press freedom serves more than the press; it encourages journalists to honor what Chafee (1947, p. 794) describes as an essential principle "too much overlooked of late": "The press is to be free so that it can give the community the service needed from the press."

PRESS FREEDOM AND PRESS RESPONSIBILITY

Neither the negative nor the positive view of liberty places a higher value on the individual or on individual autonomy. Rather, the essential distinction between the two focuses on whether the state should involve itself in bringing about the equal application of basic liberties. Under the influence of a libertarian reading of the First Amendment, journalists today—and especially their publishers—reject the positive approach to liberty on the grounds that the only proper role for the state is to protect liberty; and that the state should not venture to assess and then attempt to ameliorate the consequences of that protection. From the perspective of a negative conception of freedom, the press is under no obligation to extend its liberty or to accommodate the liberty of others. Press freedom and press responsibility, it follows, stand on opposite ends of a continuum; because responsibility ordinarily involves obligation, and because the essence of libertarianism is the denial of obligation, a "responsible press" is viewed as a contradiction in terms.

From the perspective of an affirmative understanding of the First Amendment, in contrast, freedom and responsibility stand side by side—distinct and yet inseparable. An affirmative interpretation of the First Amendment rests on the proposition that an individual's ability to gain the benefits of liberty must be included among the conditions definitive of liberty; it thus calls on the press to enlarge the opportunity for expression and to broaden its range. An affirmative theory of freedom of the press seeks to strengthen individual autonomy by acknowledging that the tyranny of private transactions poses as much of a threat to individual liberty as the tyranny of government regulation; it thus moves journalists to bring about a truly independent press, an agency of communication as free from the whims of the marketplace as it is free from the authority of the state. And an affirmative reading of the free press clause underscores the importance of public expression by recognizing its higher purpose; it thus embodies an appreciation for the role of the press, an expectation that the press will serve not just itself but the larger community whose members look to it for a clearer sense of who they are, where they are going, and where they have been.

From the perspective of an affirmative understanding of the First Amendment, in short, the journalist's principal and overriding responsibility is to assure the integrity of the press by seeing to it that the press is at all times free to conduct itself in accordance with its highest ideals. At the very lest, this means that a free press is a press free to act with regard for—and with reference to—the general welfare of its community; it means, as the American Society of Newspaper Editors recognized more than a half century ago when it promulgated its "Canons of Journalism," that freedom of the press means freedom "from all obligations *except that of fidelity to the public interest.*"

Although it is not within the province of the state to define the "public interest" at a level that would involve content-specific demands on the press, it is within the province of the state to define "the public interest" at a level that would advance the goals and values of the First Amendment. After all, the state not only created the First Amendment; it created the mechanism for its periodic interpretation. The First Amendment *is* the state's commitment to freedom of expression, and only cynicism amuck would view the state as unfit to enact its own commitment. It is logical and quite reasonable to expect the state to create incentives for responsible journalism by promoting and facilitating the widest possible application of the First Amendment. The state can legitimately foster its own conception of "the public interest"—and, by so doing, foster its own conception of a responsible press—so long as its efforts support, and not abridge, the right of self-expression.

What is not entirely clear, however, is how successful the state can be until and unless the judiciary exhibits greater sympathy for a positive view of liberty. While the primary initiative in affirmatively promoting freedom of the press may come from the legislative or executive branches of government, as Emerson would prefer, ultimately the courts must contribute as well by creating a new body of legal doctrine. Ultimately, that is, the courts must recognize that protecting the right of self-expression requires something more than simply forbidding suppression by the state; that it requires the state to support, promote, and facilitate the means of expression; and that it requires the state to protect its citizens against nongovernmental suppression of expression.

On occasion, of course, the judiciary has done just that—it has acknowledged, in the words of Justice Hugo Black, that "freedom of the press from governmental interference under First Amendment does not sanction repression of that freedom by private interests" (*Associated Press v. U.S.,* 326 U.S. 1, 20 [1945]). In fact, perhaps the strongest statement in favor of an affirmative interpretation of the First Amendment came from the Supreme Court in 1969 in its *Red Lion* decision, which upheld the constitutionality of the Federal Communications Commission's requirement that broadcasters provide individuals with time to reply to personal attacks. Citing the importance of the "right of the public to receive suitable access to social, political, esthetic, moral, and other ideas and experiences," the *Red Lion* Court enunciated a rather novel construction of the First Amendment when it ruled that it "is the right of the viewers and listeners, not the right of the broadcasters, which is paramount" (319 U.S. 190, 217 [1969]).

Red Lion today, regrettably, stands as mere dicta—more an eccentricity of the Warren Court than an enduring contribution to First Amendment jurisprudence. It is telling that in 1974 in *Miami Herald v. Tornillo,* a case involving the constitutionality of a newspaper right-of-reply law, the Supreme Court rendered a decision without a single reference to *Red Lion.* Even in the area of broadcasting, where the courts have long recognized broadcasters' "enforceable public obligations," the logic of *Red Lion* endures the ignominy of neglect. A 1981 Supreme Court decision concerning the FCC's commitment to diverse entertainment programming, for example, relegated *Red Lion* to a mere footnote and left the Commission free to use "market forces" as the only protection for the "paramount right" of listeners and viewers to receive "suitable access" to a broad range of programming (see *FCC v. WNCN Listeners Guild* 101 S.Ct. 1266, 1278, n.44 [1981]). Now with the Supreme Court's tacit support, the FCC can move ahead with plans to equate the "public interest" with the "public's interest" (see Fowler and Brenner, 1982), a policy quite appealing to broadcasters whose standing in the marketplace can only benefit from a regulatory agency that chooses to view competition among broadcasters, not diversity among broadcasters' programs, as the goal of the First Amendment (see Glasser, 1984).

On another front, however, the battle to gain recognition for an affirmative theory of freedom of the press may find considerable support from the Supreme Court. In *PruneYard Shopping Center v. Robins* (100 S.Ct. 2035 [1980]), which dealt with a conflict between the property rights of a shopping mall owner and the speech rights of individuals using the mall to solicit signatures for a petition, the Supreme Court affirmed a California Supreme Court decision that interpreted its state constitution in terms more expansive than a traditional reading of the First Amendment would allow. In its narrowest sense, *PruneYard* held that state courts may interpret state law as authorizing individuals to express themselves in a shopping mall, regardless of the mall owner's preference to the contrary. But the broader implications of *PruneYard* may portend an era of state—as opposed to federal—protection for the opportunity for expression; for the logic of *PruneYard* suggests that where state constitutions create an affirmative right of free speech, unlike the mere restriction on state action found in the First Amendment, state courts can legitimately protect their citizens from not only public but private abridgment of expression (see Note, 1980: 179).

The sympathies of the judiciary notwithstanding, much can be done by journalists themselves to combat the deleterious consequences of a libertarian view of press freedom. With or without support from the courts, modest but important progress can be made through the collective efforts of reporters and editors—efforts designed to challenge the unabashedly self-serving view of the First Amendment that equates press freedom with property rights. Through their unions and professional associations, journalists can begin to question the limits of their independence; indeed, they can begin in their own newsrooms, where press freedom ordinarily exists only at the sufferance of investors, owners, or their appointed functionaries (see Schwoebel, 1976).

But no doubt journalists will need to turn to the state when it comes to the kind of substantive reform necessary to transform the prerogatives of a private press into a press committed to the principles of democracy. For only the state can affirm the importance of a free press by protecting the press from private as well as public abuse. Only the state can restore confidence in the press by insulating the press from influences inimical to the highest ideals of American journalism. Only the state can honor the First Amendment by assuring its application. Journalists may lead the way, but in the end only the power of the state can challenge the awesome economy of the press.

Owners of the press, of course, will denounce any action by the state that might diminish their power and dominance. And they will at every turn employ the First Amendment in their defense, just as they have tried, largely unsuccessfully, to use the First Amendment to defend their campaigns against child labor legislation, the Federal Trade Commission, the Social Security Act, the Fair Labor Standards Act, and a variety of other efforts by the state to impose on the marketplace a modicum of fairness and equity. Predictably, owners of the press will cite Jefferson's preference—given the unlikely choice—for a nation of only newspapers as opposed to a nation of only government, but they will forget to mention Jefferson's great faith in the authority of the state: "I hope we shall crush in its birth the aristocracy of our monied corporations which dare already to challenge our government to a trial of strength, and bid defiance to the laws of our country" (quoted in Shattuck & Byers, 1981, p. 383).

Owners of the press will continue their battle against press responsibility, or render the idea meaningless by reducing it to the realm of each individual's conscience, because a responsible press means a press truly free to set its own agenda. A free and responsible press represents a real and substantial threat to owners because it threatens to extend press freedom beyond the privileges of property.

Perhaps what owners fear the most is that the First Amendment can be used to strengthen the bond between press freedom and press responsibility by applying the constitutional admonition against abridgment of speech and press, as Barron (1967, p. 1656) puts it, "to the very interests which have real power to effect such abridgment." It must be painfully obvious to the owners of the press that the beneficiaries of an affirmative interpretation of the First Amendment include everyone but those whose profits depend on portraying the state as the only "enemy" of a free press.

NOTES

1. The concept of ideology is applicable to the study of law when law is studied with regard for the association between ideas and interests. Accordingly, the "ideology of law" denotes "the connection between ideas, attitudes, and beliefs, on the one hand, and economic and political interests, on the other" (Hunt, 1985, p. 13).

2. I am indebted to Wolfgang Hoffmann-Riem for this conceptualization.

3. I am borrowing liberally from Gerald MacCallum's (1967) interpretation of Isaiah Berlin's (1969) distinction between negative and positive liberty.

REFERENCES

Bagdikian, B. H. (1983). *The media monopoly.* Boston: Beacon.

Barron, J. A. (1967). Access to the press: A new first amendment right. *Harvard Law Review, 80,* 1641-1678.

Barron, J. A. (1969, March). An emerging first amendment right of access to the media? *George Washington Law Review, 37,* 487-509.

Barron, J. A. (1973). *Freedom of the press for whom?* Bloomington: Indiana University Press.

Berlin, I. (1969). *Four essays on liberty.* New York: Oxford University Press.

Chafee, Z. (1947). *Government and mass communications* (Vol. 2). Chicago: University of Chicago Press.

Commission on Freedom of the Press (1947). *A free and responsible press.* Chicago: University of Chicago Press.

Emerson, T. I. (1970). *The system of freedom of expression.* New York: Random House.

Emerson, T. I. (1977). Colonial intentions and current realities of the first amendment. *University of Pennsylvania Law Review, 125,* 737-760.

Emerson, T. I. (1981, Summer). The affirmative side of the first amendment. *Georgia Law Review, 15*, 795-849.

Fowler, M. S., & Brenner, D. L. (1982, February). A marketplace approach to broadcast regulation. *Texas Law Review, 60*, 1-51.

Gillmor, D. M., & Barron, J. A. (1984). *Mass communication law* (4th Ed.). St. Paul, MN: West.

Glasser, T. L. (1984, Spring). Competition and diversity among radio formats: Legal and structural issues. *Journal of Broadcasting, 28*, 127-142.

Held, V. (1984). *Rights and goods.* New York: Free Press.

Hunt, A. (1985). The ideology of law: Advances and problems in recent applications of the concept of ideology to the analysis of law. *Law & Society, 19*, 11-37.

Kairys, D. (1982). Freedom of speech. In D. Kairys (Ed.), *The politics of law.* New York: Pantheon.

Lippmann, W. (1955). *The public philosophy.* New York: Little, Brown.

MacCallum, G. (1967, July). Negative and positive freedom. *Philosophical Review, 76.*

Machan, T. R. (1983). The petty tyranny of government regulation. In T. R. Machan & M. B. Johnson (Eds.), *Rights and regulation.* Cambridge, MA: Ballinger.

Machan, T. R. (Ed.). (1982). *The libertarian reader.* Totowa, NJ: Rowman and Littlefield.

Merrill, J. C. (1974). *The imperative of freedom.* New York: Hastings House.

Milton, J. (1927). *Areopagitica.* New York: Payson & Clarke. (pub. orig. 1644)

Note. (1980, November). Private abridgment of speech and state constitutions. *Yale Law Journal, 90*, 165-188.

Nozick, R. (1974). *State, anarchy, and utopia.* New York: Basic Books.

Owen, B. M. (1975). *Economics and freedom of expression.* Cambridge, MA: Ballinger.

Pool, I. S. (1983). *Technologies of freedom.* Cambridge, MA: Belknap.

Royster, V. (n.d.). *The right to be irresponsible.* University of Iowa, mimeograph.

Schauer, F. (1982). *Free speech: A philosophical enquiry.* New York: Cambridge University Press.

Schwoebel, J. (1976). *Newsroom democracy: The case for independence of the press.* Iowa City: Iowa Center for Communication Study (University of Iowa).

Shattuck, J.H.F., & Byers, F. (1981, Fall). An egalitarian interpretation of the first amendment. *Harvard Civil Rights - Civil Liberties Law Review, 16*, 383.

Stewart, P. (1975). Or of the press. *Hastings Law Journal, 26*, 632-637.

Smith, J. A. (1981, Summer). Freedom of expression and the marketplace of ideas concept from Milton to Jefferson. *Journal of Communication Inquiry, 7*, 47-63.

6

SOCIAL RESPONSIBILITY, REPRESENTATION, AND REALITY

Everette E. Dennis

Any evaluation of the ethical conduct of mass media organizations or the people who work for them ought to be measured against the purposes of freedom of expression. In the United States, freedom of speech and press exists as a matter of public policy for at least two compelling reasons: First, it is thought that a free press (or media system) can provide an unfettered flow of information about public affairs; and second, it is thought that the press (or media) should be a forum for differing opinions and ideas. In recent years, there has been much debate about whether these rights to freedom of expression are primarily for individuals or for the institutions of mass communication.

Into this picture comes the concept of "representation." As society has grown larger and more complex, an increasingly smaller proportion of the population is able to have its own newspaper, magazine, or broadcast station. Thus legal scholars, courts, and media critics have spoken of the press or mass media as the "necessary representative" of the people, their "trustee" or "surrogate."

This notion is not new. Indeed, the press as a "Fourth Estate" or a "fourth branch of government" predates the American revolution, tracing its origins to Thomas Macauley, who wrote that "the gallery in which the reporters sit [in parliament] has become a fourth estate of the realm."[1] For many years, however, this idea was more rhetoric than legal reality. Still, some journalists have embraced the quite contradictory notion that the press was indeed a sort of fourth branch of government, having a check and balance function, much like the other branches of government, but with no direct, legal responsibility for anything. To such commentators, there is absolute freedom on one end of the continuum and repressive censorship on the other. Thus they have argued that the press under such a system does not have an affirmative responsibility to do anything. Indeed, even some jurists have said that the Constitution of the United States does not and cannot command the press to be fair or reasonable or impartial. Still, anyone who knows the law also understands that with all rights come duties, whether anyone likes it or not.

The debate described above is often contradictory and confusing, yet it is easy to see how such positions might have arisen. Journalists and broadcasters rightly believe that they are running a business like no other business in America because they have a constitutional franchise. To them, freedom of the press means gathering information without constraint, using professional skills to shape it into news reports, and, finally, disseminating the result of this work to the audience. Media people in their heart of hearts would like to have the foregoing description of their activities accepted by the American people. But it is not that simple. Sometimes people object to news-gathering tactics, disagreeing with the way reporters do their work, with their seeming intrusion of privacy, with their manner and methods. Similarly, individuals may object to the way that a news report is written, challenging whether it is fair and accurate, whether it presents a true portrait of the event or issue under scrutiny. People might even question whether a particular report should be printed or broadcast at all. Such complaints lead to grievances, most of which never go further than private conversations with one's friends or associates, but some of which end up in the courts.

Without always articulating it precisely, what people seem to be saying is as follows: "You (the press) have special freedoms granted to you by the Constitution. That's a right. All rights have corresponding duties and your duty is to provide a flow of information and opinion that serves the public interest." Such an argument suggests that if the media are acting as "public representatives" portraying themselves as quasi-public servants (with commercial reality, of course), there ought to be some standard of accountability, one that is compatible with the liberty of the press.

What of the concept of representation and the mass media? Does the press really "represent" anyone, that is, does it "stand for" or "represent" the concerns of the public? Because press freedom in the United States is largely what the courts say it is at any moment in time, it is useful to look to judicial decisions for a better understanding of the press as a representative of the people. In a number of cases where the press argued that it should have access to public trials or prisons or other public proceedings that every member of the public clearly could not attend, courts have established a doctrine that Anthony Lewis (1979, p. 595) calls "First Amendment exceptionalism." What's behind this doctrine? Clearly, the concept of representation. For example, Chief Justice Burger, rarely regarded as a media cheerleader, nonetheless has recognized that "instead of acquiring information about trials by first hand observation or by word of mouth from those who attended, people now acquire it chiefly through the print and electronic media" (*Richmond Newspapers, Inc. v. Virginia,* 1979). "In a sense," he wrote, "this validates the media claim of functioning as surrogates for the public." In an earlier case, Justice Lewis Powell wrote,

> The people must therefore depend on the press for information concerning public institutions. . . . The underlying right is the right of the public generally. The press is the necessary representative of the public's interest . . . and the instrumentality which effects the public's right. (*Saxbe v. Washington Post Co.,* 1974)

From the legal perspective, beginning in 1966 and continuing to 1985, there are frequent references to the press as the representative of the people in cases at the state and federal level.[2] The notion is endorsed in both majority and minority opinions with justices ranging from the populist absolutist Hugo Black to the more conservative Warren Burger making reference to representation with little qualification. The jurists may disagree about when and under what circumstances representation should be invoked to give the press rights that average citizens do not have, but few doubt that the press has a special function under the Constitution and that this justifies the trustee, surrogate, representative designation.

Although acknowledging that this interpretation of the First Amendment is becoming more common, Anthony Lewis (1979) argues that a preferred position for journalism under the Constitution might have inherent dangers:

> The press is not a separate estate in the American system. Its great function is to act for the public, keeping government accountable to the public. And it would be a poor bargain, for the press and the country, if a

special status for journalism were accompanied by greater latitude for government to avoid accountability by closing its proceedings.

Worrying that the media depend on public understanding and support, Lewis quotes Robert Bork's statement, "To the degree that the press is alone in the enjoyment of freedom, to that degree its freedom is imperiled." Former Justice Potter Stewart (1975) is even more adamant. In a much quoted speech at Yale Law School, he observed that "the primary purpose of the constitutional guarantee of a free press was . . . to create a fourth institution outside the Government as an additional check on the three official branches. The relevant metaphor," said the justice, "is the metaphor of the Fourth Estate."

It is not surprising, of course, that when faced with lawsuits challenging their performance, the media will invoke any argument that might help them win their case. Thus it has been argued that the pronouncement of media lawyers and news executives in trials when they make "Fourth Estate" claims is really not pertinent to the day-to-day activities of reporters. There are two reasons why this is not the case. First, reporters and editors do invoke the "representation argument" in their day-to-day activities, unconnected to court decisions and the musings of worldly philosophers. Second, the indirect basis for much reporters' behavior is based, in part, on an understanding of their rights under the law. If Supreme Court justices not particularly known for their love of media are agreeing that the institutions of the press have a "representative" function, who are reporters to disagree?

First, day-to-day activities. In the smallest hamlet and the largest city, reporters play a kind of informational guerilla warfare game with public officials, business leaders, and other individuals. Some information obviously flows cooperatively from news sources to the media, but some does not. Public officials wanting to manage information that makes them look good may not want an enterprising reporter to reveal embarrassing facts. Members of a school board negotiating delicate salary or personal issues with an employee may also thwart inquiries for detailed information. People in the private sector—for example, corporate executives who control local payrolls—may not take kindly to a business reporter who wants to do a story on their corporate strategy that delves into the relationships between middle and top managers. The reporters in these and other situations say, "I want this information for my readers." And quite often, they will also say, "And I'm entitled to it because there is a right to know." The so-called right to know, which has no direct constitutional origin (Dennis & Merrill, 1984), is often cited in relation to the concept of representation.

If such a right exists (and about that there is genuine dispute among scholars, jurists, lobbyists, the press, and others), it does so only because the press has a quasi-representative role. Thus reporters rightly object when they are barred from meetings of public bodies that discuss public business. Why? Because they believe that they are there to "represent the public." Of course, there is also the assumption that all members of the public are legally entitled to be present, but the room won't hold them, or they choose not to attend, and so on. Therefore, says the journalist, I'll be there. I'll represent you and your interests by covering the meeting and delivering the news via newspaper, radio, or television. Battles between public officials and the media over public meetings and public records could fill volumes. This is not a distant, theoretical consideration, but the stuff of day-to-day journalistic practice. Reflecting on this in a speech to the American Society of Newspaper Editors, John Hughes wrote, "Editors grandly proclaim that their newspapers represent the people. They believe this. On the best newspapers this is true. But this declaration requires that newspaper editors account to the public for what they do in their name [and] far too few do this, at least do it effectively" (Dennis, 1980).

All of the discussions about the right to enter a public meeting, and other local disputes, would be little more than incoherent shouting matches if it were not for the courts. Not infrequently, reporters, editors, and others who are thwarted in their efforts to get information serve notice that they believe that they (or their organization) are legally entitled to such information, whether that means entry to a trial or an accounting of public monies paid to a private firm. They will (and have) initiated lawsuits to get information, articulating a theory of representation to justify their claims. Similarly, the media also use the representation argument when they defend themselves against those who say that they overstepped their bounds, that they intruded on privacy, or used proprietary information inappropriately. "We're entitled to do this," say editors and broadcasters, "because we represent the public and the public has a right to know."

Stepping back from the legal and journalistic debate, it is fair to ask where the concept of representation comes from and how it relates to the press. The notion of one person representing another has ancient origins that surfaced in Greece and Rome; it has also occupied the attention of scholars who use it as an intellectual tool to examine the role and purpose of government. How is it, they ask, that one person can represent others? By what process do some individuals have a legitimate (or illegitimate) claim that gives them such authority? The underlying idea of representation, of course, is that of "stand-in." Because some individuals cannot or do not wish to act on their own behalf, they designate someone else, a representative, to take their desires and wishes and "re-present" them.

In modern society, this representative role is usually left to governmental institutions. However, political scientist Hannah Pitkin (1972, p. 2) has written, "Institutions and practices which embody some kind of representation are necessary in any large and articulated society, and need have nothing to do with government." Because most of the discussion of representation typically centers on government, Pitkin's comments are especially useful in looking at the role of the media as representatives of the people. Not incidentally, the scholarly debates over representation that stretch back at least to Plato and include such commentators as Hobbes, Rousseau, Burke, and Mill most often involve the nature of representation on the one hand and the relationship of the representatives to their constituents on the other.

When one considers the nature of representation, for example, there are different metaphors that can be employed; for example, such images as "picture," "map," "mirror," and "sample." Some representatives simply try to draw a map; that is, they chart out the territory and select the main features. Still others construct a picture that may even be somewhat abstract, focusing on one aspect of information coming from the constituents. The sample metaphor involves scientific selection. One tries to systematically select enough from the whole to represent it accurately. What does all this have to do with the mass media? As I have written elsewhere:

> To the extent that the press is a conduit between the organized institutions and interests of society and the public, it is representative. Most commonly in definition of representation, a surrogate figure stands for or acts for someone else. Representation is not a self-contained end in itself, but part of a larger process. The most common definition of the term is making present in some sense something which is nevertheless not present literally or in fact. While the representational problems of the press may not be directly analogous to those of representative government, studies of representation as a political concept can be useful in unraveling what might otherwise be a conceptual thicket. (Dennis, 1979)

How might the representation metaphors actually work when applied to media organizations? Each of the following presents a "picture" of society:

- *The New York Times*
- *The Wall Street Journal*
- *The National Enquirer*
- *The CBS Evening News*
- *Cable News Network* or C-Span
- *USA Today*

The New York Times provides a comprehensive record of the day's news, sometimes even including the verbatim texts of important presidential speeches and highly detailed coverage of the stock market. *The Wall Street Journal*, on the other hand, presents a business-oriented perspective on the nation and the world, selecting those news items of specific business or economic interest. *The National Enquirer* brings a sensationalistic picture that focuses on the bizarre and the unusual. *The CBS Evening News* is known for a highly selective presentation of national and international news. All of these media outlets portray society, representing the world to their readers and viewers. Does anyone really provide an exacting "photograph" of news and public affairs? Perhaps not, although the *Cable News Network* (CNN) or C-Span come close when they carry gavel-to-gavel coverage of an important trial or congressional hearing. As for samples, a paper with a penchant for coverage of demographic trends, such as *USA Today*, tries to employ social survey sampling to cover such issues as housing in America.

The courts have moved slowly toward some kind of accommodation with the "representative role" of the press; they have as yet not developed a coherent theory of representation that can be used consistently to resolve disputes between the media and various individuals and institutions that claim grievances. Perhaps they never will because the legal system responds to specific grievances rather than persuasive social issues or theories.

Members of the press, like the courts, are of two minds on the representation idea. They use the concept of representation in a rhetorical and a legal sense when it is useful to them. However, when they are confronted with standards of conduct that might be used to evaluate their performance, they quickly avoid representation. They reject the application of ethical standards, even those they have developed or become signatory to, such as codes of ethics and fair trial-free press guidelines, saying that there is no legal requirement that they exercise fairness. Editors and broadcasters will generally acknowledge a voluntary moral obligation, however.

The unwillingness of the media to guarantee a fair or representative view of society is at odds with the Commission of Freedom of the Press that, in its final report in 1947, urged, "The need for the citizen for adequate and uncontaminated mental food is such that he [or she] is under a duty to get it." It was the Hutchins Commission that introduced the idea that the press is obliged to give a "representative picture" of the various constituent groups that make up society.

Many journalists would agree in principle with the "representation picture theory," but would object if they were personally criticized for not covering a particular group or some aspect of the local community. Violations of the representative picture theory by the press include newspapers that have ignored minorities or women, for example, even though they make up an important part of the local community and the media-consuming audience.

The concept of representation, which is quite useful in several different contexts, has been used to evaluate the representativeness of the content of the media: Does it reflect the community and the most salient and pertinent issues for society? It has also been used to address the representatives of the personnel of the media: Do news organizations, for example, have staffs that are reflective of the gender and ethnic makeup of the community they serve? In both areas there is much dispute. There is no agreement about who should decide whether content is representative or not. However, on the matter of representative staffs, media organizations have been more amenable. Many have professed interest in hiring minorities and women, although their track record by their own admission is less than impressive.

It would be unfair to leave the impression that the representation issue is something that lies only in the purview of scholars, jurists, and media executives. Debate over the subject of representation with regard to the public is usually summed up in one frequently heard statement: "Who elected you anyway?" The idea that the media are self-styled representatives of the public wrankles many citizens who have spoken out about the arrogance of the press in purporting to represent the people. This point of view was at the heart of the criticisms of former

Vice-President Spiro Agnew in the 1960s when he delivered stinging attacks on the media. It was also on the minds of Richard Nixon, when he appealed to a "silent majority," and Ronald Reagan, when he embraced the "moral majority." These alleged constituencies were said to take issue with the media. Reporters, it was said, surely did not represent them or their views. In recent years, the "nobody elected you" position has been mentioned in connection with television coverage of hostages and in the occasional interference in foreign policy by network news through interviews with chiefs of state outside of official diplomatic channels.

A question arises about who is right. Is the press really the representative of the people or is it a usurper, a self-appointed representative pushing its own point of view rather than that of its constituents or advertisers? The answer is that the representative role of the press is part of an ongoing bargaining game between the American people and their media, with helpful (and sometimes not so helpful) intervention by journalists, judges, politicians, and philosophers. Certainly, in a mass society, the media do provide a basis on which information is channeled to the people. It is often information that the people do not have the resources to get on their own. Thus, in a sense, Dan Rather and his correspondents are our representatives in the various capitals of the world as they serve as the public's "eyes and ears." We count on them for a representative account of the day's news (albeit abbreviated) and assume that we aren't getting a distorted view that will impair our ability to act as responsible citizens. Of course, even Walter Cronkite used to say, "For more information consult your local newspaper."

The basis for at least part of the representative claim also seems well founded. There is surely constitutional authority for freedom of the press, which has come to mean not only dissemination of information but also gathering it and packaging it into some kind of coherent form and format. This the media do under the mantle (some say it is a cloak) of freedom of expression.

The concept of representation, which is very old indeed, is still a new idea in the context of media freedoms. It is a useful and sometimes troubling concept. It is with us though, not because scholars are pushing it but because the media invokes it and courts have sanctioned its application as never before. It is likely to generate lively arguments for years to come.

NOTES

1. The origins of the term "fourth estate" to describe the press are somewhat controversial. Most often the idea is attributed to Edmund Burke who, according to Thomas Carlyle in *Heroes and Hero Worship: The Hero as a Man of Letters* (1839), wrote, "Burke said there were Three Estates in Parliament; but, in the Reporters' Gallery yonder, there sat a Fourth Estate more important far than they all." Because the statement is not found in Burke's published works, it is now believed that Carlyle inadvertently attributed the phrase to Burke rather than Macauley, who mentioned it in his "Essays: Hallam's Constitutional History," tenth paragraph from end, *Edinburgh Review,* September 1828. The three estates of the realm in France were the clergy, the nobles, and the burghers. Lawyers there were called "the fourth estate."

2. In addition to cases previously cited, see *Pell v. Procunier* (1974) 417 U.S. 817; *Nebraska Press Assn. v. Stuart,* (1976) 427 U.S. 539; *Houchins v. KQED,* (1977) 438 U.S. 1; *First National Bank v. Bellotti* (1978) 435 U.S. 765; *Gannett Co. v. De Pasquale* (1979) 443 U.S. 368; *Globe Newspaper Co. v. Superior Court* (1982) 457 U.S. 596—all Supreme Court decisions; *U.S. v. Criden* (1981) 648 F. 2d. 814; *Belo v. Clark* (1981) 654 F. 2d 423; *Application of the Herald Co.* (1984) 734 F. 2d 93; *First Amendment Coalition v. Judicial Inquiry Review Board* (1984), 579 F. Supp. 192—all federal court cases; and *State of Montana v. District Court* (Mont. 1982) 654 P. 2d 982; *Miami Herald Publishing Co. v. Lewis* (Fla. 1982) 426 So. 2d 1; *Florida Publishing Co. v. Morgan* (Ga. 1984) 322 S.E. 2d 233; and *Kerns-Tribune Corp. v. Lewis* (Utah 1984) 685 P. 2d 515—all state cases.

REFERENCES

Commission on Freedom of the Press. (1947). *A free and responsible press.* Chicago: University of Chicago Press.

Dennis, E. E. (1980, Autumn). Touchstones: The reporter's reality. *Nieman Reports.*

Dennis, E. E. (1979). The rhetoric and reality of representation: A legal basis for press freedom. In B. Rubin (Ed.), *Small voices and great trumpets: Minorities and the media.* New York: Praeger.

Dennis, E. E., & Merrill, J. C. (1984). *Basic issues in mass communication.* New York: Macmillan.

Lewis, A. (1979). A preferred position for journalism?. *Hofstra Law Review, 7* (3).

Pitkin, H. F. (1972). *The concept of representation.* Berkeley: University of California Press.

Richmond Newspapers, Inc. v. Virginia. (1979). 448 U.S. 555.

Saxbe v. Washington Post Co. (1974). 417 U.S. 843.

Stewart, P. (1975). Or of the press. *Hastings Law Journal, 631,* 26.

7

REPORTING AND THE OPPRESSED

Clifford G. Christians

After two years of heady debate, the Commission on Freedom of the Press published its report, *A Free and Responsible Press*, in March 1947. Henry R. Luce of Time, Inc., financed the inquiry with a $200,000 contribution to Robert Maynard Hutchins, celebrated president of the University of Chicago. Hutchins assembled 13 of America's notables for 17 meetings to hear 225 interviews and 58 testimonies and to study 176 documents. What we call the "social responsibility" theory of the press emerged from this potent mixture.

Instead of facilitating the interests of business or government, the Hutchins Report insisted on the media's duty to serve society. Believing that the press was caught in the mystique of its own individual rights, the Commission stood both terms on their head with the label *social responsibility*. The complications of postwar America, in the Commission's view, demanded more "truthful, comprehensive, and intelligent" reporting than was generally available from a press preoccupied with independence from government and co-opted by the demands of profit.

Students of the media know this history well, but they remain ambivalent about its meaning and importance. Is social responsibility just a pleasant slogan like the "people's right to know?" Does it introduce anything different from the Jeffersonian model in which the enlightening newspaper is our national glory? Could it betray the press's First Amendment protection? And—perhaps the overarching question—how is society defined? Presuming my primary duty is directed "out there," to whom am I obligated really? Because "society" is an amorphous term, one might ask, does it merely refer to readership or audience? If broader than that, does social responsibility still make sense?

A Free and Responsible Press provides clearer boundaries than its detractors generally recognize. Certainly it refers euphemistically to the press as a public forum "for exchanging comment and criticism" and for "clarifying society's values and goals." But more concretely, this report insists that the modern media "present a representative picture of society's various groups" (p. 2). Although that demand does not exhaust the meaning of social responsibility, it remains in my mind a central component. The instinct of the Hutchins Commission was correct on this score, and I endorse it in this chapter as a first-level generalization. Along with *A Free and Responsible Press* as a whole, this requirement of presenting a "representative picture" continues to be a good idea but in search of a theoretical foundation. From my perspective, social responsibility theory remains a frail reed because it is perceived largely as timid neoliberalism.[1]

In what follows, I provide a justification from social ethics for the press's responsibility to "all social categories without stereotype." In the process, what the Commission dimly felt becomes a stronger, philosophically interesting concept. It takes a more radical turn while gaining normative status as a necessary though insufficient condition of responsible reporting. I will defend the proposition that justice for the powerless stands at the centerpiece of a socially responsible press. Or, in other terms, the litmus test of whether or not the news profession fulfills its mission over the long term is its advocacy for those outside the socioeconomic establishment.

Admittedly, to argue that reporting must be an instrument of social justice raises complicated issues about the nature of the press's structure as presently conceived in democratic societies. Although I do not treat all the problematics in what follows with the detail they deserve, I am not thereby dismissing such matters as insignificant. So-called objectivity, First Amendment freedom, government watchdog, and other professional values are distinctive contributions of the Anglo-American tradition and this chapter does not challenge their merit.

For the present assignment, I hold the news media's feet to the fires of injustice and suffering. In our day of persistent inequalities, do the most vulnerable receive priority or not? I elaborate on this responsibility below, not because it exhausts all the daily activities of stations or newspapers but because it is their meaning-center nonetheless. Speaking generically, one might ask, how does the news operation score on this most stringent test? With presidents, prime ministers, governors, and mayors closing down mental health offices, boarding up the welfare centers of North America, and withdrawing food stamps, who will be a voice for the unemployed, Appalachian miners, the urban poor, Hispanics in rural shacks, the elderly, women discriminated against in hiring and promotion, ethnic minorities without opportunity in a land once seen as flowing with milk and honey?

Life is immensely demanding for the press of late. How can it remain upright while the Western world downsizes its economy? Although the times have grown more painful, I assert the strongest possible mission for the news profession: Does it promote justice? Does it aid in fulfilling the stirring vision in which justice flows down like a mighty stream? In a day when the powerless have few alternatives left, and virtually no recourse, should the press not serve as a voice, as a megaphone of sorts for those who cry out to be heard? Shouldn't the communications media be the channel of today's impoverished, so their complaints and pleas for mercy will rise above the noise of a busy and complicated nation?

POWERFUL AND POWERLESS

In confronting the question about news and social justice, one can point with pride to the media's record on civil rights. The press reached in the 1950s for the brass ring and made it. Remember the Sheriff O'Connors loose in the land: "Only you and me, black boy. It is 2 a.m. Nobody is looking. Guess who will win?" The press entered the arena and put those Bull O'Connors under pitiless publicity until the court of opinion shamed them into silence. One might reasonably ask whether white pro-Martin Luther King activists arrested in the rural south during the civil rights struggle could have survived unless reporters for the wire services, networks, and major newspapers had not openly told their story. On the whole, concluded Nicholas Herrock, a reporter for the Baltimore *Sun*, "Prosecutors, police, and other mechanisms of law enforcement spent much of their time and effort . . . endeavoring to conduct their business with as little public scrutiny as possible" (Rivers, Schramm, & Christians, 1980, p. 78). News reporters crusading for open courts, insisting on civility from the police, and advocating access to the voting booths were essential in breaking down a condemnable system.

Or remember migrant workers in the wake of civil rights marches. As Chet Huntley retired to the Big Sky country from NBC news, his proudest memories were NBC's crusade for the Latino migrants abused in the groves of Florida. Notable moments, indeed, in the advance of justice. The list is long. Cameras there at Selma, complicitors in the cause, until Black Power took on meaning and the beleagured minority began receiving legal parity. It is such a shining record on civil rights that one could conclude that the press met the most stringent test regarding justice.

But we must probe more deeply. Before a 1954 Supreme Court ruling set the civil rights struggle in motion, the American press largely ignored the issue of race. In point of fact, Martin Luther King was

> the chief reason for television's fascination with the substance of the civil rights movement. He was eloquent, capable of high pronouncements and dramatic persuasive appeals, and thus became a critical rhetorical figure in television's discourse. . . . As the first black leader to galvanize thousands with his own rhetoric during television's maturity, his judgment of television's importance for the movement was crucial to black consciousness. (Asante, 1976)

King's brilliance proved more significant in bringing a coalescence between television and minorities than did a compelling desire by newspeople to engender social and economic justice.

In like manner, much of the media's concern has always been in *Sixty Minutes* style, kamikaze ethics. Cameras capture the stony gaze of a lonely old woman, abandoned in a nursing home rocking chair, and the audience is touched. But the substructure—the institutional evil that allows this abuse of the aged—remains virtually unreported. The press diligently covers the sensational. As Arnoldo Torres (1985) laments, for example, the Hispanics recently elected as mayors, as governor of New Mexico, and as representatives to Congress are placed in the limelight, but there remains "a general lack of critical analysis of our political development" in such areas as immigration, education, business, and party politics (p. 11). A simplistic definition of newsworthiness—"man bites dog"—leads the media to the boiling cauldrons; when there are open flames reporters catch fire. However, "The poor are poor all the time. It is not journalism's ordinary business to deal with the unstartling normalities of life. Reporters need a *story*, something shapely and elegant. Poverty is disorderly, anticlimactic and endless" (Rosenblatt, 1984).

Throughout the civil rights movement—as with other issues—the press has been largely reactive, requiring visible emergencies to spur it to action. In fact, given their dependence on news coverage, one could argue that civil rights activists were constantly forced into increasing escalation—sit-ins, marches, demonstrations, confrontations, and riots—in order to maintain publicity. In this sphere and regarding the news function as a whole, Peter Jacobi (1979, pp. 28-29) inquires,

> The quieter problems—are they getting in-depth investigative attention? Schools in drift. Hospital room shortages and surplusses. Medical school admissions procedures today impacting on the kind of doctors we have tomorrow. Soaring interest rates and what they mean to the little man. Joblessness and the minority young. Energy sources and environmental dangers. Landmark designation versus business district rejuvenation. Middle-income housing shortages. Urban parks development. Proposition 13 when there is no surplus.

The close observer certainly celebrates the achievements. Robert Maynard is an effective voice for training nonwhite journalists. UPI developed an intensive study of Chicago's slums and its "FHA-financed segregation." There are more than 200 black publishers, and some have thriving and influential newspapers and magazines. The Arizona *Daily Star* once provided a sensitive and intelligent 28-page section, "Tucson's Barrios: A View from Inside," on life in Chicano ghettos. The National Newspaper Publishers Association has demonstrated creative leadership in editorial policy for its black newspapers—such assistance being vital because black-run papers are not automatically free of racism and require greater maturity themselves in advocating social justice. The *Chicago Tribune* during 1985 featured a front-page series, "The Millstone," on the underclass.

However, as the Kerner Commission (U.S. National Advisory Commission on Civil Disorders) charged in 1968 and the U.S. Civil Rights Commission in 1979, there has been little long-term reporting of our social underbelly that leads to political literacy regarding human rights. Instead, one sees burnout at present, a general weariness with the struggle. Rather than promoting the critical consciousness that undercuts institutional racism, many news professionals continue to have greater enthusiasm for chasing fire trucks and for bludgeoning errant public officials into submission. Minority coverage is still sporadic, and generally disappointing; there are a few bright spots, but these are exceptions to the long record of failure.

Meanwhile, the challenges are immense because the problems of the 1980s differ qualitatively from those of the 1960s:

> The axis of press issues has shifted since the days when black Americans had to demonstrate for the right to ride in front of a bus, sit at a lunch counter, or use a bathroom. The challenge of the 1960s was to crack the color barrier in the press corps and to report the movements for social and economic justice. Today the struggle in journalism is over a second generation of issues: tokenism in employment (as intolerable today to minorities as was exclusion in the sixties), and inaccurate, inadequate portrayal of minority communities (even less excusable than was total neglect years ago). (Kotz, 1979)

The first-generation issues lent themselves to a visual medium, springing as they did from beatings in the streets and the charismatic King. But contemporary problems are not so easily reported. Being more obtuse than ever, they cannot be reduced as readily to the television screen, do not bring reporters running, and Martin Luther King is dead.

Regardless of lessons in civil rights activity from another decade, what about the news profession and social justice now? The discussion must begin with the glaring disparity between big power media on the one side and the powerless on the other—two ill-fitting shapes, not synchronized and, in fact, incompatible.

Students of American history know what happened as the nineteenth century closed and the twentieth began. Steel, cities, manufacturing, inventions, immense natural resources, and a dynamic capitalism turned the United States into an industrial nation. American culture crossed a watershed into the era of big business. Mass communications took on a giant industrial character too—Joseph Pulitzer and William R. Hearst in newspapers, AT&T and Western Union in electronics, Cyrus Curtis (*Ladies Home Journal* and *Saturday Evening Post*) in magazines. From then until today, the media have had to struggle to keep free from the pressures of big business so that they can serve society more responsibly.[2]

Since this cataclysmic period, the media have been largely big business. Many media properties are now owned by diversified conglomerates that rent cars, manufacture food, and mine copper in addition to managing their information holdings. Several such corporations—RCA and Gulf & Western, for example—are among the world's largest. There is a decided trend toward concentration in the newspaper industry; 70 papers die or go into the hands of chains per year. Today, 96% of American cities with daily newspapers have only one publisher. One study predicts that fewer than two dozen firms will own all the dailies by the 1990s (*The Washington Post*, 1977; Bagdikian, 1983). The Gannett Company, for example, already owns more than 80 dailies in 30 states. No wonder Aleksandr Solzhenitsyn (1978, p. 838) lamented,

> The press has become the greatest power within Western countries, more powerful than the legislature, the executive, and the judiciary. One would then like to ask: By what law has it been elected and to whom is it responsible?

This course toward concentrated ownership has led to serious discussions outside the industry and soul searching within it, as to whether a gigantic mass media system can effectively promote political literacy rather than serve stockholders, money, and absentee landlords. As Donald MacDonald (1976, p. 16) has argued in his provocative essay,

> Today, the business of media is very big and very profitable. The compulsion to grow bigger and more profitable, while understandable— though often unattractive—in say, the oil, steel, and automotive industries, introduces a profound conflict of interest in the media and invites hypocrisy in media owners whose function, as A. J. Liebling once noted, is "to inform the public, but whose role is to make money."

The late Lord Thomson, Canadian entrepreneur, apparently once said, "I buy newspapers to make money to buy more newspapers to make more money. As for editorial content, that's the stuff you separate ads with" (Bagdikian, 1977). Most owners are not that crude, but conglomerates own media businesses primarily as a way of enlarging product lines for the purpose of revenues. There is little incentive to use profits for expanding news coverage, except in the few remaining places where competition demands it. Broadcasting stations do not exist primarily to produce programs but to produce audiences that can be sold to advertisers. The temptation, then, is to avoid unpopular themes that might reduce subscribers or audiences, and to shrink news budgets for cheaper fare. Some owners do infuse new dollars into their outlets and expand services, but far too many seem to operate only in terms of their profit-and-loss statement. And local needs easily become forsaken if dividends can be increased elsewhere. Why not put a cheap game show on TV rather than a locally produced program, and depend on wire copy rather than local reporters if both cost less and are reasonably acceptable to the audience? Richard Reeves (1978, pp. 10, 14) is understandably searing in his attack on the merger trend, using the Gannett Company as an illustration:

> The future is as visible as McDonald's Golden Arches. Gannett and McDonald's are in the same business—and that business is not causing trouble. . . . What Gannett is doing is training a cadre of managers with one charge: maintain the corporation's dazzling growth rate. . . . When the cops do break into most American newsrooms, they're not going to find much more than wedding announcements and PTA bulletins.

Watch the rhetoric, and media companies often refer of late to papers or stations as "products" or "units," and budgets are called "profit plans."

These misgivings about big power media refer to systemic features, of course. Some media outlets are not baldly rich. There are papers and stations and reporters who keep the wolf at the door, who refuse the arrogance of power, and seek justice with the vigor of the prophet Jeremiah. In certain cases, reporters self-consciously separate their own purposes from a management preoccupied with finances. Pulitzer prizes are still awarded, by and large, to professionals who distinguish themselves for public service and who shun careerism and big dollars. In public broadcasting, the McNeil-Lehrer Report, and National Public Radio's "Morning Edition," and "All Things Considered" frequently probe deeply into events. Ted Koppel's "Nightline," journals of comment and opinion, and the ethnic press often enhance political literacy. Occasionally local papers rise to the occasion and carry through a penetrating series on a community problem. *Time* magazine on April 30, 1984, selected ten great newspapers on the grounds of their community contribution rather than profit margins. One realizes that too often the apathetic public refuses serious work and prefers sensationalism. Obviously there are exceptions and the public is blameworthy too. But for those who claim civic literacy as the press's occupational norm, the big business mentality is a nettlesome demonic force nonetheless.

Recently the *Los Angeles Times* declined to start a Hispanic edition, even though one-fourth of the city's population now speaks Spanish. The paper had spent $1.5 million the year before in a special edition for its southwest suburban readers. There were net profits of $96 million that year, yet management decided in the negative. Economic deprivation of Hispanics, it concluded, does not make them attractive enough to advertisers who market products for the affluent. Despite his paper's distinguished leadership in most respects, the publisher Otis Chandler excused its commitment to the city's ethnic cultures with a typical put-down: "It's not their kind of newspaper. It's too big, . . . too complicated" (Gutierrez & Wilson II, 1979).

In that sense, Chandler reflects a weakness in the standard urban big-capital newspapers and broadcast units of the United States. Earl Shorris (1977, p. 110) provides this caustic analysis of Chandler's award winning counterpart on the opposite coast, for example:

> The *New York Times* escapes its responsibility by staying away from home. A reader of the *Times* can be comfortable in . . . a city where over a million people have nothing but welfare payments to keep them alive, and where entire neighborhoods have been burned out or left to rot. . . . Only at Christmas do the poor appear in the *Times*, and even then they are only cases, without the names and faces that invade dreams. . . . In that tradition, the *Times*, for all its far-flung correspondents, isolates its readers from the real world, permitting them to pursue virtue in their island lives, enabling them to believe in social justice while living in an unjust society.

Big-power media tend to forge alliances with hegemonic interests that preclude meaningful advocacy for the defenseless. During a recent period, for instance, the "Phoenix Forty" included the top executives of the city's five largest banks and Arizona's biggest employers. Among these elites were the chief executive officers of the major papers and broadcasting stations. Whose families and pet projects received constant coverage? There is no evidence that "Phoenix Forty" businesses were ever brought to task when they polluted, or discriminated in hiring, or reneged on service (Rivers et al., 1980, p. 110). Or take the Mississippi Power and Light Company of Jackson—the state's largest utility. MP&L spends $500,000 annually advertising in the local papers, and the one owner of both papers sits on MP&L's Board of Directors. Is anyone surprised, then, that a $30 million rate increase request is given front page coverage with no opposing points of view (*More,* 1976)? In Champaign-Urbana, Illinois, the owners of the paper and major radio and television stations move in a circle of bank presidents, law firm partners, and business owners. Meanwhile they cover the safe beats at city hall and the police station, but rarely probe the recesses of the city, the suffering and untutored (De Long, 1982).

These illustrations ought not be misunderstood. I am not accusing these media of outright collusion, deliberate racism, or conscious restraint of trade. I agree with Harvey Molotch (1979, p. 76), who argues that the pressures originate deeply within journalism training itself:

> The reporter's "nose for news" includes as a critical component the sustenance of the ruling class. This nose has been subtly shaped through a complex array of mechanisms and institutions: political science, which teaches future news reporters that the power and influence structure of the United States is reflected in the organizational chart of governmental institutions; economics, which teaches the same people that . . . prosperity is best measured by such indexes as GNP; sociology, which teaches them to make a fetish of fact, to ritualize objectivity, and to see the poor as a source of human interest stories but not as a class with potentially insurgent behavior and goals.

My concern is with a pernicious commercial and establishment motif that can subtly undermine the news profession's commitment and service to the community. Classical democratic theory establishes for the press a crucial role; education and information are the twin pillars on which a free society is said to rest. This place of privilege—guaranteed by the First Amendment—entails that the press fulfill a much grander mission than those businesses that manufacture widgets and market pet rocks. Informed public opinion is a weapon of enormous power, indeed, the cornerstone of legislative government. Therefore, the press can be appropriately urged to surpass its own financial interests out of particular special obligation to the public.

William Allen White—an outstanding editor himself—once complained,

> Too often the publisher of an American newspaper . . . is a rich man seeking power and prestige. He has the country club complex. The

business manager of this owner is afflicted with the country club point of view. . . . Therefore it is hard to get a modern American newspaper to go the distance necessary to print all the news about many topics. (Commission on the Freedom of the Press, 1947, p. 59)

Robert Hutchins protested in similar terms to the American Society of Newspapers Editors: "If the soliloquy [of the publisher] is that of one of the richest man in town, it is more likely that it will sound the same political note as other soliloquies in other towns, rendered by other rich men" (Rivers et al., 1980, p. 110). Although generally not cut off from the world of racial and economic minorities to the same degree as management, the structure itself, the pressures of group-think, the lack of rewards, and the natural deference toward employers typically co-opt working reporters also. The latter find it extraordinarily difficult to remain inspired by the preferences, sentiments, and anxieties of the disadvantaged. How else does one explain the tragedy that for more than a year agencies such as World Vision pleaded unsuccessfully with the networks to cover drought-stricken Ethiopia? Jacques Ellul (1978) legitimately castigates the left for ignoring the "truly poor" and promoting the "interesting poor" who serve party goals. Unfortunately, in its own way, the culture of news gathering tends toward a similar distinction, dramatizing the poor whenever they serve the conventions of reporting.

Ethnocentrism is another dimension of the same problem. Given the dominance of middle-class values within American news operations, a nearly unbridgeable gulf ordinarily separates them from the enclaves across cultural, linguistic, social, political, prejudicial, or geographical barriers. According to one line of analysis, 16,700 culture groups around the world are locked away from the mainstream of their societies. These hidden peoples exist without recognition or adequate representation: 600 separate tribes with a population of more than 5 million in the Latin American lowlands, 60,000 Chinese families in Mozambique, one million Turkish guest workers in the German Federal Republic, the Japanese "Little Tokyo" in Los Angeles, Urdu-speaking Muslims who are residents of the Punjab in India. Indigenous Indian tribes—the Miskitos—along the Caribbean coast of Nicaragua have been totally ignored by Somosa and must struggle for even a hearing from the Sandinistas. In the United States alone, more than 1.5 million aliens become residents annually. A University of Chicago study concluded that 20 million Americans belong to the so-called fringe religious cults such as Hare Krishna and the Moonies. In the last census, 75 million Americans classified themselves as members of 120 different ethnic subcultures (Dayton, 1979; Dayton & Wagner, 1983). The malady of ethnocentrism prevents this rich panorama from taking shape in our consciousness.

In 1973, television became the primary weapon at Wounded Knee on South Dakota's Pine Ridge Indian Reservation. In a ten-week siege, 200 activists from the American Indian Movement (AIM) brought before the nation an array of grievances pent up inside after years of humiliation and oppression by the Bureau of Indian Affairs. Two Indians died of gunshot wounds and a federal marshal was paralyzed from the waist down. The media were co-opted as an instrument of confrontation politics.

Dennis Banks of AIM complained afterward, "I told the newsmen, 'We don't care if you totally condemn us, but please convey the real reasons why we're here.' We held briefings every day so the television people wouldn't just take pictures of the weapons and the trenches. But TV coverage went largely to the battle action anyhow." And Ramon Roubideux, a Sioux Indian lawyer, added, "Only the sensational stuff got on the air. The facts never really emerged that this was an uprising against the Bureau of Indian Affairs and its puppet tribal government" (Christians, Rotzoll, & Fackler, 1983, p. 57).

NBC's Fred Briggs made a noble attempt at clarifying the long trail of broken treaties that led up to Wounded Knee. Richard Threlkeld of CBS seemed to grasp the main issues at stake. ABC's Ron Miller provided some powerful interviews with the AIM leader Carter Camp. However, the need to encapsulate the story of Wounded Knee into two-minute slots forced reporters, on the whole, to focus on events that made good pictures. Outsiders never gained a sense of the massive oppression of Indian peoples that caused the occupation. They did not see the extensive corruption in many tribal governments. Most viewers never realized that AIM was invited to lead this protest by traditional Indian leaders at Pine Ridge who thought they had exhausted other means of protest.

Press accounts of the original Wounded Knee battle are chilling to reread many years later. "Indian Treachery" was a common headline; and "hostiles," "savages," and "desperate" were typical terms for the Indians in 1890. "News" reports regularly hailed the Seventh Cavalry as "heroes"; and the San Francisco *Chronicle*'s account concluded by quoting General Miles's "don't-be-uppity" declaration that "their severe loss may be a wholesome lesson to the other Sioux" (Marquis, 1974; Weisman, 1975).

But the 1973 coverage was not clearly elevated above the stereotyped language 83 years earlier. Of this recent return to the Wounded Knee location, a young Ogalala Sioux contended,

> The glory hounds among the press came here and wrote articles and filmed television stories about the Wild West gunfights between the marshalls and the Indians. They never did find out what caused it all, nor what if anything it accomplished. Anyway, they're gone and we're still here. (Rivers et al., 1980, p. 209)

The media were confronted by AIM in terms that news people understand—setting up bunkers and holding off the federal government with guns. But the powerless were not empowered. The voiceless were not heard speaking in their own language. Here was an opportunity to make the cause of justice inescapable, but the media did not prove equal to the task.

To this day a lengthy agenda remained unfulfilled. Most of the old, blatantly segregationist practices in media institutions have been rooted out. But morally adequate coverage of ethnic minorities and of the poor still does not exist. Robert Maynard, black publisher of the Oakland *Tribune*, continues to insist on the need for sensitive reporting in context; that is, "a protrayal of our communities as places inhabited by real people, not pathological fragments" (Rivers et al., 1980, p. 212).[3] Meanwhile, hiring and promotion practices require major renovation, with only 5.8% of all media practitioners coming from ethnic minorities according to the *1984 Report of the American Society of Newspaper Editors*. Of the nation's dailies, 61% employ no minority journalists whatsoever, and 92% have none in management positions (Guimary, 1984).[4]

Unfortunately, however, there is a decided weariness with the struggle. Formerly committed white journalists have actually become bored with changing policies and structures. A relaxing of the will seems apparent everywhere. The urgency has faded. To be transformed, this professional world needs its present coolness reinvigorated. And a long-term, urgent, well-motivated interest in justice can be sustained only among those convinced that favoring the worst-off is not merely do-goodism but an ethical imperative.[5]

ETHICAL FOUNDATION

Can a legitimate case be made that responsible news in hard times benefits the least advantaged? Is there a principle of social justice that demands a voice for the voiceless, even when such a commitment clashes with profitability or century-long conventions, and even though a fundamental restructuring of media institutions might ensue?

The most celebrated defenses of late are anchored in John Rawls's monumental (1971) *Theory of Justice*. From Rawls's perspective, fairness is the fundamental ideal in the concept of justice. And where situations are inherently unequal—as with the powerful press and muted poor—Rawls would rightly argue that averages are unfair and intuition too prone to error. Therefore, we can gain intellectual leverage from his now classic "veil of ignorance" where all parties step back from real circumstances into an "original position" behind a barrier where roles and social differentiations disappear. Participants are abstracted from such individual features as race, class, sex, group interests, and other real conditions, and are considered as equal members of society as a whole. They are men and women with ordinary tastes and ambitions, but each suspends these personality features and regains them only after a contract is in place. Behind the veil, no one knows how he or she will fare when stepping out in real life—the participants may be male or female, ten years old or ninety, a Russian or a Pole, rookie or veteran, black or white, advertising vice-president or sales representative for a weekly. As we negotiate social agreements in the situation of imagined equality behind the veil of ignorance, Rawls argues, we inevitably seek to protect the weaker party and minimize risks. In case I emerge from the veil as a beginning reporter rather than a big-time publisher, I will insist on fair treatment for the former. The most vulnerable party receives priority in these cases, and the result, Rawls would contend, is a just resolution.

From the hypothetical social contract formulated behind the veil, two principles emerge. These, Rawls declares, will be the inevitable and prudent choices of rational men and women acting in their own self-interest.

The First Principle calls for a maximum system of equal basic liberty. Every person must have the largest political liberty compatible with a like liberty for all. Liberty has priority in that it can never be traded away for economic or social advantages. Thus the First Principle permanently conditions the Second.

The Second Principle involves all social goals other than liberty and allows inequalities in the distribution of these goods only if they act to benefit the least advantaged party. The inequities in power, wealth, and income upon which we agree must benefit the worst-off members of society (Daniels, 1976).

Obviously Rawls's formulation is a powerful corrective to democratic societies prone to benefit the majority and pay only token respect to the few. The original position serves as a persuasive strategy in the middle-range for deciding in particular situations which action is morally desirable. However, Rawls's theory reaches no deeper than the democratic society it presumes. Those uninspired by such political values as individual self-interest, social contract, and negative freedom find Rawls contrived and unconvincing.

An even more secure foundation rests on the nature of being. A theory of human nature forms the root, radix, square root out of which social justice is defined—radical in the pristine sense of straight down to the source. Admittedly, a social ethics making ontological claims is itself open to dispute far beyond the range of this essay. What such an enterprise entails can only be postulated here, with its defense and elaboration more appropriate in other contexts.

Personhood is one essential characteristic of what it means to be human. In Paul Tournier's (1957) terms, real persons are knowable behind the image or appearance. Personhood means the capacity for self-transcendence, that is, the ability to rise above urges and circumstances, to will how we behave. In other words, humans are moral beings; free will entails the responsibility to maximize free will among the entire human family. Thus it is axiomatic that all human activities have a moral dimension in that they either liberate or oppress personhood.

If a primordial feature of human beings is personhood, then surely the other must be community. Human beings and communities are interdependent, separable for purposes of analysis, but never separated in actuality. As Kant argued, persons ought to be treated as ends in themselves, but they are simultaneously communal and their communality necessitates equal protection as well. Hans Jonas (1984, p. 35) speaks of an "inextricable interweaving of human affairs" in which mutuality, equality, and the fair distribution of benefits make community possible." Given this essential unity, in Paul Tillich's (1963, p. 38) terms, the reunion of the separated is the telos—the end, aim, goal—of moral behavior.

The Western liberal mind commits a fundamental error at this juncture: Societies are considered aggregates of atomistic selves, collections of automatons. With the individual rather than community as defining category, social life is a derivative, an extension less real than the individual entities that constitute it. Even the progressive liberalism that inspired the Hutchins Commission conceived of society as a collectivity, as a "heap of souls" held together on a piece of ground by contract.

Persons-in-community as the irreducible base differs radically from the individual autonomy that has dominated Western culture since the Enlightenment. However, it also stands in contrast to a socialist model in which what is real to society's members can be real only in relation to the whole and the integrating norm is the entire social organism. Nor is persons-in-community a synthesis of these two, but a fundamental reconceptualization in which historically and geographically constituted cultures form a mosaic or composite, a living organism. Therefore, in this vision, the powerless are not merely a long list of unfortunate individuals downplayed in reporting because their numbers and economic power are limited. They constitute a subculture whose grotesque rupture from the mosaic violates most starkly the communal essence.

CONCLUSION

In many respects, Bill Moyers's "CBS Reports: People Like Us," serves as a model of the type of news story coveted by the communal mind. Moyers gave a voice to Larry Ham, Frances Dorta, and Cathy Dixon—powerless people who had fallen through the safety net. Television became an instrument for those being hurt—though often unintentionally—by social policies poorly designed or ineptly administered, and in some cases blatantly unfair. Consistent with the canons of acceptable news practice, Moyers gave no moralistic preachments. He sought only to make the faces of the poor as distinct and their voices as clear as audiences typically hear and see from agents of the establishment. The result was redemptive media, mass communications honoring the cause of social justice—at least for a fleeting hour.[6]

In the print medium, Ken Auletta's *The Underclass* (1982) represents the redemptive motif. Released by *The New Yorker* staff for a two-year study of nine million unassimilated Americans caught in unshakable poverty or chronic antisocial behavior, Auletta succeeds in demonstrating that next to war and peace—and perhaps the economy—the underclass is "the most momentous story in America" (p. xviii).[7] He vacillates over questions of public policy and confuses matters of causality. His case study of the Wildcat Skills Training Center in New York tends to obscure systemic and structural dimensions. These weaknesses are endemic to the democratic liberalism and conventions of objective reporting that the book embodies. Nonetheless, *The Underclass* shows a redemptive glow in a professional world encumbered by snippets of unrepresentative events. Auletta's book-length reporting engages the consciousness of careful readers and enhances their political insight.

But obligation for reform cannot be limited to media practitioners themselves. Of course, this essay—concerned with professional reporters—has concentrated on role responsibility. And fulfilling such contract-specific duties that accrue to our jobs or capacities or expertise can never be gainsaid.[8] The battles will be largely won in the trenches. I reiterate the overwhelming need for discerning, freely rendered responsibility that flows from an activated conscience.

Schopenhauer once called the press the second hand of history— made of inferior metal perhaps, but a ticking account of space/time nonetheless. Or, in other terms, reporters are preparing a first draft of history. Because first drafts directly influence the final statement, press portrayals feed into public discourse and play a portentous role in the shape our culture and the sociopolitical realm ultimately take. In its loftiest sense, the press ought to amplify public debate and reconstitute the arguments so that it becomes an important public forum where significant issues of social justice are fruitfully raised and resolved. News reports, that is, should aid readers and viewers in understanding their *Sitz im Leben* so they will achieve greater capacity for involvement in the sociopolitical process. As a distinguished editor has summarized it,

> We (the press) are too much cop and lawyer rather than explaining fully what happened. Journalism should take the responsibility for public comprehension. Explanatory journalism is the mission of the press. Are we large enough in spirit to see it or do we just expose abuses of power? (Patterson, 1981)

Glimmers of hope appear at times, and periodically one observes concerted efforts toward purposeful history and equity in human affairs. Reinhold Niebuhr is undoubtedly correct: Institutions are characterized by a collective, self-regarding tribalism that becomes especially apparent when attacked from the outside. Institutions, however, do have a residual moral and social sense; although self-serving, they need not be categorically without redeeming value (Neibuhr, 1965, pp. 26, 68). Thus print and video news can be considered redemptive when they serve not as instruments of accommodation but of critique and social change. Documentaries, columnists, commentators, opinion journals, public broadcasting, and mass paperbacks often resonate with a redemptive accent and lobby for important ideas. On occasion, the major news weekly magazines devote special issues to high school dropouts, the 18-year-old to 34-year-old unemployables, religious groups under vicious persecution, recent immigrants fighting for legitimacy, malnourished children, prisoners, or the physically and mentally handicapped. Wilson and Gutierrez (1985) conclude that diversification in new media technology currently offers unprecedented opportunity for breaking apart homogenization.

But that does not make the story complete. Public responsibility is no less vital today. While differing significantly in kind, the contractual dimension will not long endure unless operating within the public context. In fact, these two forms of responsibility live in symbiotic relationship. The 1984 Pastoral Letter of the National Conference of Catholic Bishops condemning poverty in the United States was vigorously reported in the press and illustrates how public and professional responsibility can operate in concert. Or, to use another example, the Physician Task Force on Hunger in America issued a report in 1983 through the Harvard School of Public Health. The efforts of experts, widely disseminated by the press, enters the public domain and enables citizen awareness and action.

Public responsibility refers to the broad moral duty of non-professionals for the health and direction of their society. By definition, as cultural beings we share obligations for our life together whether or not we have institutional affiliation or specific expertise. People live in an ongoing relationship of accountability. Nonresponsibility is inconceivable. In H. Richard Niebuhr's (1963) illuminating sense, we are responsible selves set in a particular direction and responding in either an acceptable or blameworthy manner. Graham Haydon (1978, p. 51) refers to this moral outlook as an "ethic of responsibility," a view of "virtue-responsibility" required of generic humans without reference to roles. Advocates of an ethic of responsibility "treat the requirement of responsibility as an ever-present moral demand, necessarily incumbent on any person qua person (or qua moral agent) prior, logically to particular responsibilities." Certainly its exercise is conditioned by the amount of power one actually holds for making change, but in terms of a holistic understanding of humans and society, professionalism is everyone's business, though we can lay upon persons a cross no greater than they ought legitimately to bear.

In the framework of this essay on media professionals, the audience and subscriber carry a considerable burden for holding the news media accountable. Setting aside a naive libertarianism that puts all responsibility in the marketplace of ideas, it is nonetheless true that readers and viewers generally receive the fare they prefer. If the larger community would share a genuine mutual burden regarding the mission of the press and broadcasting, we could aid immeasurably in calling them to a symbolic form in which history takes on meaning for those without other avenues of participation. And lest the task appear intractable, I am reminded of Dietrich Bonhoeffer's wisdom: "In a fallen world, lay grip on the meanest edge of the dark issues and trim them into decency."

NOTES

1. That conclusion refers directly to the Report itself. However, books in the background, such as William E. Hocking's *Framework of Principle*, and commissioners such as Reinhold Niebuhr, represented more than timid neoliberalism. One of today's best students of the Hutchins Commission, Mark Fackler, sees in its work a fundamental wrestling with such critical matters as scientific naturalism and transcendentalism. (See Paul Mark Fackler, *The Hutchins Commissioners and the Crisis in Democratic Theory, 1930-1947*, Ph.D. dissertation, University of Illinois—Urbana, 1981).

2. For interpretive histories of these events, see Daniel J. Czitrom (1982, Chaps. 1-4, 6) and J. Herbert Altschull (1984).

3. Oakland Tribulations, *Columbia Journalism Review* (January/February 1983). For purposes of this essay, I concentrate on the news function. It is patently obvious, however, that the problem and solution extend to all dimensions of mass media programming. The historian J. Fred MacDonald (1983), for example, demonstrates the disenchanting trend in television entertainment recently toward visible but subordinate and stereotypical roles for blacks.

4. These figures do not include the nearly 200 black newspapers in the United States that make up the National Newspaper Publishers Association. Enabling the black press to

remain financially and editorially viable ought to be included in our social ethics agenda. With American cities increasingly black, and white papers unable to reach them, the black press could become the urban medium of the future. For an overview of the recent history, see Phyl Garland (1984).

5. Making advocacy of social justice a crucial mission of the press does entail a shift from conceiving news as the objective transmission of facts to news reporting as storytelling. News, in the view of this essay, is to be seen as a narrative art form in which the aim is telling worthy stories strongly so that the audience's conscience can be engaged. For a review of the nature and logic of contemporary attempts to develop an alternative journalism to the received view, see David L. Eason (1984). Stanley Hauerwas (1981) demonstrates the central importance of storytelling for developing community life generally.

6. Broadcast on April 21, 1982, though many CBS affiliates refused, for various reasons, to air the program; in the state of Illinois, for example, it was shown only on Channel 2 (WBBM) in Chicago. For a review of the contents, background, rationale, and available literature, see Terry Mattingly (1982), "People Like Us: South Succotash on Television," unpublished paper available from the author, Charlotte *Observer*, Charlotte, North Carolina 28233.

7. Auletta's study stands in the tradition of such books on poverty as Michael Harrington's (1961) *The Other America: Poverty in the United States*; Oscar Lewis's *The Children of Sanchez* (1961) and *A Death in the Sanchez Family* (1970); and Jacob A. Riis's (1971) *How The Other Half Lives*. However, besides the long-term poor, Auletta uses the debatable strategy of including three other groups in his underclass category: street criminals, hustlers, and traumatized drunks-drifters.

8. The famous work of H.L.A. Hart (1968) on contractual responsibility is placed in the context of professional ethics by John Ladd (1982).

REFERENCES

Altschull, J. H. (1984). *Agents of power* (Chaps. 3-4). New York: Longman.

Asante, M. K. (1976, Autumn). Television and black consciousness. *Journal of Communication*, pp. 137-141.

Auletta, K. (1982). *The underclass*. New York: Random House.

Bagdikian, B. (1977, March/April). Newspaper mergers in the final phase. *Columbia Journalism Review*, pp. 17-22.

Bagdikian, B. (1983). *The media monopoly*. New York: Harper & Row.

Christians, C., Rotzoll, K., & Fackler, M. (1983). *Media ethics: Cases and moral reasoning* (p. 57). New York: Longman.

Commission on the Freedom of the Press. (1947). *A free and responsible press*. Chicago: University of Chicago Press.

Czitrom, D. J. (1982). *Media and the American mind: From Morse to McLuhan*. Chapel Hill: University of North Carolina Press.

Daniels, N. (Ed.). (1976). *Reading Rawls: Critical studies of a theory of justice* (Part III, pp. 169-281). New York: Basic Books.

Dayton, E. (1979). *That everyone may hear: Reaching the unreached.* Monrovia, CA: World Vision International/MARC Division.

Dayton, E., & Wagner, P. C. (1983). *Unreached people: Unfinished business.* Elgin, IL: David C. Cook.

De Long, R. (1982, January/February). Down, minions, down! *Columbia Journalism Review, 20*(5), 47-49.

Eason, D. L. (1984, March). The new journalism and the image world: Two modes of organizing experience. *Critical Studies in Mass Communication,* pp. 51-65.

Ellul, J. (1978). *Betrayal of the west* (Trans. Matthew J. O'Connell) (pp. 82-125). New York: Seabury.

Garland, P. (1984, September/October). The black press: Down but not out. *Columbia Journalism Review,* pp. 43-50.

Guimary, D. L. (1984, Winter). Ethnic minorities in newsrooms of major market media in California. *Journalism Quarterly, 61*(4), 827-830.

Guiterrez, F., & Wilson, C. C., II. (1979, January/February). The demographic dilemma. *Columbia Journalism Review, 17,* 53-55.

Harrington, M. (1961). *The other America: Poverty in the United States.* New York: Penguin.

Hart, H.L.A. (1968). *Punishment and responsibility.* New York: Oxford.

Hauerwas, S. (1981). A community of character: Toward a constructive Christian social ethic (Chaps. 1-4). Notre Dame: University of Notre Dame Press.

Haydon, G. (1978). On being responsible. *Philosophical Quarterly,* pp. 46-51.

Jacobi, P. P. (1979, January). Abuse, abuse, abuse. *Quill,* pp. 28-29.

Jonas, H. (1984). *The imperative of responsibility: In search of ethics for the technological age* (p. 35). Chicago: University of Chicago Press.

Kotz, N. (1979, March/April). The minority struggle for a place in the newsroom. *Columbia Journalism Review,* p. 24.

Ladd, J. (1982). Philosophical remarks on professional responsibility in organizations. Pp. 191-203 in A. Flores (Ed.), *Designing for safety: Engineering ethics in organizational contexts.* Troy, NY: Rennsalaer NSF Study.

Lewis, O. (1961). *The children of Sanchez.* New York: Random House.

Lewis, O. (1970). *A death in the Sanchez family.* New York: Vintage.

MacDonald, D. (1976, November/December). The media's conflict of interests. *The Center Magazine,* pp. 15-35.

MacDonald, J. F. (1983). *Black and white TV: Afro-Americans in television since 1948.* Chicago: Nelson-Hall.

Marquis, A. (1974, May/June). Those 'brave boys in blue' at Wounded Knee. *Columbia Journalism Review, 13,* 26-27.

Molotch, H. (1979). Media and social movements. Pp. 71-93 in M. Zald & J. D. McCarthy (Eds.), *The dynamics of social movements.* Cambridge, MA: Winthrop.

More (1976, April). Fowl play, pp. 5-6.

Neibuhr, R. (1960). *Moral man and immoral society.* New York: Charles Scribner's Sons. (pub. orig. 1932)

Neibuhr, H. R. (1963). *The responsible self.* New York: Harper & Row.

Neibuhr, R. (1965). *Man's nature and his communities.* New York: Charles Scribner's Sons.

Patterson, E. (1981, January). Seminar at Hastings Center Conference on Ethics and Journalism, Hastings-on-Hudson, NY.

Rawls, J. (1971). *A theory of justice* (pp. 3-53, 118-192). Cambridge, MA: Harvard University Press.

Reeves, R. (1978, August 1). The press's great threat. *Esquire*, pp. 10, 13.

Riis, J. A. (1971). *How the other half lives.* New York: Dover.

Rivers, W. L., Schramm, W., & Christians, C. (1980). *Responsibility in mass communication* (3rd. Ed.). New York: Harper & Row.

Rosenblatt, R. (1984, July 2). Journalism and the larger truth. *Time*, p. 88.

Shorris, E. (1977, October). Cutting velvet at the New York Times. *Harper's*, p. 110.

Solzhenitsyn, A. (1978, July 7). A world split apart. *National Review*, p. 838.

Tillich, P. (1963). *Morality and beyond* (p. 38) New York: Harper & Row.

Torres, A. (1985, July 2). Perspective: The struggle of the Hispanics. *Chicago Tribune*, sec. 1, p. 11.

Tournier, P. (1957). *The meaning of persons* (Trans., Edwin Hudson). New York: Harper & Row.

The Washington Post (1977, July 13-August 4). The newspaper business. Business and Finance Section.

Weisman, J. D. (1975, September/October). About that 'ambush' at Wounded Knee. *Columbia Journalism Review, 14*, 28-31.

Wilson, C. C. II, & Gutierrez, F.(1985). *Minorities and media. Diversity and the end of mass communication.* Beverly Hills, CA: Sage.

PART III

Practicing Responsible Journalism

The authors in this last section step away from theorizing about the notion of responsibility and step away from competing press theories. These chapters consider how responsible journalism might look in specific situations.

Linsky offers a new model for how the media ought to be responsible in reporting on government. What happens when it is clear that the press is doing more than simply reporting the news? What happens when it is clear that the traditional adversarial relationship between press and government is nothing more than a myth? Linsky argues that media understanding of their participatory function is the only answer along with media acceptance of the responsibilities implicit in that new role

Isn't the small town press different from media operating in metropolitan areas? Aren't we doing journalists and their audiences a disservice in measuring journalistic responsibility against a big city model? Ziff issues a resounding "yes" to both of these questions and presents a model for responsible journalism that allows media representatives to be part of the community rather than simply on the outside reporting what they see within.

8

PRACTICING RESPONSIBLE JOURNALISM: PRESS IMPACT

Martin Linsky

Late in 1979, senior officials at the Environmental Protection Agency decided to do something about the public perception that the government was not acting decisively enough about the problems of hazardous waste.

A task force was formed. Its mission, according to Jeffrey Miller, then Acting Head of the EPA's enforcement division, was "to affect legislation, and to try to turn the press around from criticism of the agency's handling of the hazardous waste problem to acceptance that the agency was doing what it could, but lacked all the tools it needed." One of the first products of the work of the task force was a lawsuit filed on December 20, 1979, by the Department of Justice on behalf of the EPA against Hooker Chemical, the city of Niagara Falls, the Niagara County Health Department, and the Board of Education of the city of Niagara Falls. The suit asked for $124.5 million, for an end to the discharge of toxic chemicals in the area surrounding Love Canal, and for cleanup of the site and relocation of residents if necessary.

Because proving damage was essential to establishing Hooker's liability, in January the lawyers at Justice and the EPA agreed to do a quick "pilot study" to look for chromosomal damage among Love Canal residents, evidence of exposure to toxic chemicals. They chose people who would be most likely to show damage—those who had already exhibited some possible manifestations, such as people with cancer or children with birth defects. There would be no control group, but if the results looked "promising" they planned to go ahead with a full-blown rigorous scientific investigation that could be used in the case. None of the senior administrators at the EPA was aware of the pilot study; the political, legislative, and public information arms of the agency were uninvolved.

Around the first of May, the consultant doing the study phoned the EPA to report that he had found chromosomal aberrations in 12 of the 36 people tested. In a confirming letter sent shortly thereafter, he noted that the findings were "believed to be significant deviations from normal, but in the absence of a control population, prudence must be exerted in the interpretation of such results." He recommended that the larger study be undertaken. EPA officials began to evaluate the study and decide what to do next.

On Friday, May 9, EPA and Justice officials briefed Jane Hansen of the White House staff. Hansen was an aide to Jack Watson, who was secretary of the cabinet and assistant to the president for intergovernmental affairs (and in the process of becoming chief of staff in the White House). Notes taken at the meeting quote a Justice Department lawyer saying that the EPA was "leaky," and that the study would not stay out of the press for long. By the following Thursday, May 15, a few reporters were making general inquiries at the EPA, which suggested that they knew something about the study, if not anything more than its existence. Becoming concerned, Hansen that day wrote a long memo to Watson in which she said that she feared that "momentarily the press/media will have the results" of the study. She recommended that the administration "take the offensive *quickly* in announcing the results of the studies ourselves." She urged that they say that officials would verify the data within a week, which would "provide us with some flexibility and give us a week to answer some important questions and determine our course of action."

The memo had the desired effect. Watson called a meeting for Friday "to get to the bottom of the situation." He was concerned, he recalled recently, "with the public's perception, not so much the public at large, but the public that was directly affected . . . I was very concerned about wrong, rumor-filled, distorted information getting to them through the press."

The meeting was held at 11:00 a.m. on Friday, May 16, in Room 248 of the Old Executive Office Building. Senior administrators from all of the agencies involved were invited. Notes from the meeting indicate that the decision was made to inform the study subjects immediately and to hold a press conference the next day, Saturday, to release the study results and announce the federal response. Representatives of the Justice Department argued for a Friday press conference, but the need to inform the study participants first of what their own tests showed was deemed to be an overriding consideration. Wednesday was set as the day for making the next decision.

Then, someone leaked information. That afternoon, the *New York Times* called the EPA looking for comment to include in the story it was running on Saturday about the pilot study.

The Saturday morning news included most of the information the government was planning to release at the press conferences. Irwin Molotsky's story, on page 1 of the *Times*, attributed to "federal officials" who "asked not to be identified" the results of the study. The story strongly suggests that the leak did not come from the EPA, but did originate with someone who knew of the press conference plans. The article quoted a Hooker spokesman criticizing the release of the study, emphasizing the preliminary nature of the findings and expressing concern that the publicity would cause panic among Love Canal residents.

The government was in a difficult position, trying to disseminate pretty horrible-sounding results while stressing their tentative nature and the need for verification. The situation was further complicated by the leak. By the time of the press conference, the government's chief news—the study itself—was already old news for the reporters. They used the press conference to try to advance the story. The new news was made in response to reporters' questions, not in the government's prepared statement releasing the findings of the study. On the question of relocation, EPA Deputy Administrator Blum said that a decision would be made "probably by Wednesday." On the question of who would pay for relocation, she was quoted as saying, "We certainly can't let money stand in the way." She characterized the results of the study as "alarming."

In the Sunday *New York Times* there were four Love Canal-related stories, including two on page 1. The press conference made the CBS and NBC nightly news. It was a national story. The networks had given it coverage, and the primary regional newspaper, the *Times,* has a national readership. The subject tapped anxieties shared by people everywhere. The coverage continued, with the networks devoting a substantial amount of time to reporting every twist and turn in the Love Canal story for the next few days.

Watson had informed the president about the Love Canal press conference in a memo that seemed to anticipate that events were already moving ahead of the policymaking plan:

It appears that the residents face an immediate health hazard that demands speedier response than litigation . . . Justice and I did not feel that we could conceal the information until [Wednesday, when the study would have been evaluated] . . . people will have to be moved when validation is in . . . I . . . will attempt to avoid a lengthy public battle resulting in no action and growing hysteria among Love Canal residents.

It did not take long for the hysteria to manifest itself. The residents of Love Canal were fanning the flames, in part for the benefit of the attendant press. On Monday, they engaged in a little friendly hostage-taking, holding two EPA officials for several hours. New York Governor Hugh Carey was doing his part, publicly criticizing the federal government's handling of the situation and calling for a fully federally funded relocation.

By early Tuesday it became clear to Watson and Hansen that this boil had to be lanced. They remember stopping to talk between the White House and the Old Executive Office Building. Watson said something like "I think these people have been jerked around enough . . . we'll just have to go ahead." The decision was made.

At a Tuesday White House meeting, government scientists argued in vain for more time to assess the relationship between the chemicals and the health risk, an attitude Watson characterized as "writing a scientific treatise on the head of a pin." It was too late. The discussion turned to what needed to be done to prepare for a relocation announcement the next day, Wednesday.

At that point, government officials still had not established that there was legal authority to pay for relocation, no one knew where the money was coming from if the authority existed, negotiations with Carey on sharing the costs had not been completed, and the results of the review of the study were not in. Yet on Wednesday, Barbara Blum held another press conference, this one to announce that the administration was reversing its long-standing policy and would relocate 710 families from the Love Canal area.

The review of the pilot study was completed that day. It concluded, as have other studies since then, that there was "inadequate basis for any scientific or medical inferences from the data (even of a tentative or preliminary nature) concerning exposure to mutagenic substances because of residence in Love Canal." In the ten days beginning on the Friday before the first press conference, there were 31 separate articles in the *New York Times*, including eight front page stories and three editorials. Network news programs devoted 31.5 minutes to the story during that period, the equivalent of an entire evening news program, a substantial amount of time for them.[1]

What happened here?

When journalists and government officials have been asked that question they have come up with two very different answers. Most journalists argue that the reporters were was just doing their jobs, reporting the facts and letting the policymakers do the rest. The press, they say, was simply exercising one of its most important roles, namely, that of keeping government decision makers' feet to the fire. That view imagines the press as standing outside of the policymaking process, observing what is going on and telling the people what happened.

Government officials see it another way. To them, the press forced the Carter administration into disrupting the kind of rational, deliberative decision-making process that is essential to good government. Barbara Blum was talking about both the process and the result when she said some years afterward that the relocation was "the worst public policy decision during my four years with the government." She remembers feeling during the period between the two press conferences as if she were "standing in a field and being pelted with five hundred balls." Most of the balls were being lobbed by the press. This view suggests that the press is an adversary.

Neither seems right. The press was neither outside of the policymaking process nor was it adversarial to it. By its sheer presence, the press was an integral element in the judgment to go ahead with the Love Canal relocation. The media were a continuing factor in the story, as a function of their aggressively performing the basic responsibilities of journalism as they understand them to be: finding out what was going on and reporting it. Officials had to deal with a horde of reporters in and around the government, covering the news, looking for stories, asking questions, seeking leads, doing their jobs.

The press was pervasive. What the media did had a significant impact on what the officials did. For example, the media augmented if not supplanted normal channels of communication. For Watson, Hansen, and the others, the pressure they were getting to act was the result of messages being conveyed to them through the media from Carey, from the residents of Love Canal, and sometimes in editorials and in the prominent placement of news stories, from the press itself. The government officials used the press to send messages back, although they tried to deal directly as well. They preferred to talk in person to those most centrally involved, but they found themselves unable to do so to their satisfaction, in part because Carey and the residents found it more powerful to speak to the administration through the press.

The leaked Friday story on the pilot study also had a special impact. It threw the government's game plan out the window, and significantly affected both the substance and the speed of the policymaking from that point forward. The purpose of the press conference changed. What had been designed to announce the study became, in Barbara Blum's words, an effort at "mitigating the damage" by showing that the federal government was in control and taking steps that were both responsive and responsible.

Take the press out of the Love Canal relocation decision and at the very least the step to relocate would have been taken more deliberatively; perhaps it would not have been taken at all. The press was neither separate from the process nor adversarial to it.

The self-image of the press as being distant from the arena and outside of the process of government decision making is as much a myth as the officials' views of the press as adversary. These romantic notions are no longer true, if they ever were, but both sides cling to them because they mask more complicated realities. They bear little relation to the way officials and reporters deal with each other in the real world. They die hard because policymakers and reporters have an interest in keeping them alive.

For the official, the adversary idea is a way to explain bad press without accepting any responsibility for it. Negative coverage is attributed to irresponsible reporters and news organizations who just want to sell papers or get high ratings, not to faulty decision making or ineffective leadership on the part of the official.

Similarly, for the journalist, the idea of distance is a way of asserting independence in the face of enormous interdependence. On the whole, today's journalists do not want to see themselves as part of policymaking because they do not want the responsibility for the impact their reporting has on government. Their own ethic demands that they report on government—not, in anything more than the most passive sense, be a part of it. Not only do recent history and tradition in the journalism business, such as the value on objectivity, drive them to that position, but the consequences of understanding their influence are complicating. If they know the impact of what they are reporting and publishing in a specific case, then they may be said to have contributed to and be held partially responsible for the result.

Hard as it is to kill off the notions of distance and adversariness, it is important to do so. Notice that even though the notions are dearly beloved by their adherents, they cannot coexist: it is difficult to picture the press being distant and adversarial at the same time. By perpetuating the myths, both sides suffer in their communications and relations with one another, and both sides suffer in their credibility with their publics. For the media, it is a significant challenge to bring their image of themselves and their conduct into harmony with reality because much of what is valued about a free and democratic society rests on a credible press.

These ideas about distance and adversariness did not suddenly appear out of thin air. They evolved as the relationship between officials and news organizations has evolved throughout American history. Richard A. Schwarzlose (1983) of Northwestern University has described three phases of that relationship.[2] In the first phase, which lasted until the Civil War, newspapers were partisan and enjoyed a close relationship with government officials. Newspapers were often started to serve the interests of specific parties, politicians, or causes. Those in power bestowed financial benefits and prestige on their newspapers, and the newspapers in turn served the officials' political and policy interests.

The second period began after the Civil War and lasted for a hundred years. The dominant factor in the press-government relationship was the transformation of most newspapers from partisan organs appealing primarily to their own loyalists to mass market publications designed to appeal to everyone and offend no one. The norm became objectivity, a notion that gained eminence as a commercial principle designed to increase circulation and gain advertising revenues as a result, but that soon became internalized as an editorial virtue as well.[3] There was muckraking and yellow journalism during this era as well, but the notion of the press as a source of independent neutral information for the public was the overriding ethic. It was not until the McCarthy period in the 1950s that it began to be clear that officials could use journalists' deference to the false god of objectivity to their own advantage. It was not until the next decade, however, that the Vietnam War put to rest the norm of objectivity in the relations between the press and government.

Schwarzlose's third phase of press-government relations is characterized by the notion of adversariness. Clearly there were examples of an adversary relationship between officials and reporters as the nation struggled through the ordeals of Vietnam and Watergate. News

organization formed investigative teams designed to root out government malfeasance. Journalists took pride in demonstrating their new
skepticism toward politicians and policymakers, which often bordered
on cynicism. Officials began to look at reporters as the enemy,
questioning their professionalism, honesty, and loyalty.

If that third phase was difficult and intense, it also did not last very
long. There is nothing in the Love Canal relocation story that suggests
that kind of hostility. Yet in many respects, that interaction of reporters
and officials is characteristic of the press-government relationship
today. The techniques of the interaction were conventional: press
conferences, leaks, and a lot of telephone calls from reporters to officials
asking questions and seeking information. The impact was substantial.

The relationship between the press and government today has
entered a new phase, which might be described as institutional. The
press is a pervasive force in policymaking. What is reported and how it is
reported has a huge impact on the people, processes, and policies of
government. These are the inevitable conclusions from current research,
anecdotal material, and personal observations. They are confirmed by a
recent three-year study I was privileged to direct at the Institute of
Politics at Harvard University's John F. Kennedy School of Government, which examined just how the press affects policymaking in
Washington.[4]

Overall, that study found that the press and policymakers in
Washington are engaged in a continuing struggle to control the view of
reality that is presented to the American people. The engagement is
highly competitive, but collegial nonetheless. When the media's view
and the official's view are more or less shared, the struggle is more like a
waltz. When there is a wide gap, or when early on in a particular issue it
is not clear which perspective will predominate or even what the
perspectives are, toes are stepped on and there is tension between the
partners. In either event, the interaction is important to both
policymakers and reporters because they believe that the stakes—the
goals of governing and the ideals of journalism—are so high.

Everywhere we turned in that research—case studies of particular
policy decisions, a survey of all senior officials from the last twenty
years, and extended interviews with a group of senior policymakers
selected by a panel of their peers as having been particularly distinguished in their jobs—we found evidence of how central the press is to
the decision-making process in government. As Robert McNamara
said, before his government experience he believed that "all you had to

do was figure out the right thing." He learned, however, that "you also have to figure out how to explain it to the public." Over 96% of the senior federal policymakers we surveyed said that the press had an impact on federal policy, and over half of them considered the impact substantial.

Part of the explanation for this is that everywhere policymakers turn in Washington there are reporters to deal with. Journalists are there, doing their jobs, asking questions, looking for information. The dramatic increase in the number of Washington-based journalists has extended the reach of the press deeper into the bureaucracy and added to the number of reporters covering those policymakers who were already well-covered. Policymakers simply cannot avoid the media; as a result of the sheer presence of the press, policymakers' jobs are different from what they otherwise would be. Because the press is such a presence, policymakers spend a lot of time thinking about and dealing with press matters. They use the press to explain themselves to colleagues and constituencies, and to learn what other officials and groups are thinking about them and their programs. They understand that what the press covers and how it covers the news can affect their policies, the way they do their jobs, and their careers. As a consequence, for many policymakers managing the press has become an integral part of their professional routine. Sometimes, as at certain points in the Love Canal story, press considerations are so much a part of policymaking as to be indistinguishable from it.

The waltzing couple does not precisely capture the way reporters and officials interact because it suggests that they are on the same plane and have the same stakes in public affairs. That is certainly not the case. Officials have direct interests in policymaking. They stand to gain or lose—personally, professionally, programmatically, and productively. The press has a different stake, a stake in the process itself. Reporters and officials are not partners in policymaking. They do different jobs. They have different interests. Journalists usually do not have personal and professional stakes in the outcomes of policy debates. They are more like stockbrokers who care less whether or not the market moves up or down than whether or not it is moving. Their stake is not in a particular policy result, but in the continuing story . . . and in the story continuing.

The relationship is more like a Greek chorus, if you will pardon the somewhat esoteric metaphor. A student of mine made that suggestion after a lecture in which I was fumbling around trying to find a metaphor that worked. Typically, the chorus in Greek drama shared the stage with the actors, but could not make set speeches. Sometimes its members talked directly to the audience, reporting, interpreting, and commenting on what the actors were saying and doing. Sometimes they represented the audience to the actors, half in and half out of the action. Sometimes, although rarely, the chorus itself became the subject of the story. Although the chorus members could not make a set speech or be advocates, they often interacted with the actors by way of questions and answers, often with the questions designed to make a point or elicit information the actor preferred not to reveal. The chorus never directly revealed its motive. Sometimes it was the confidant of the actor, and sometimes the actor swore the chorus to secrecy; in either of these cases the chorus gave up its primary function as the mediator between the audience and the actors. The actors often spoke to the audience and to each other through the chorus. The challenge for the poet was always to keep the chorus within its sphere and yet a vital force in the action.

Whether or not the mid-1980s press-government relationship can be best understood in terms of Greek drama, the Harvard study did confirm that it is very different than it was twenty years before. A spirit of cooperation used to characterize the way reporters and officials interacted. Reporters relied on officials, and trusted their information. And the reverse was often equally the case. For example, reporters regularly offered advice to presidents, sometimes at the initiative of the White House and sometimes even complimenting him in print if the advice was accepted.[5] Nothing better manifests that attitude than the famous story of the willingness of James Reston of the *New York Times* to ask his editors in New York to modify the paper's article on the government's preparation for what became the ill-fated Bay of Pigs invasion of Cuba in 1961. At the president's request, Reston urged the editors to take the story off the front page and to eliminate any references that would suggest that the invasion was imminent. They complied, and the rest is history.

President still ask newspapers and television networks not to run stories, and often the news organizations still agree. But they do only after great internal angst and after making an independent judgment that lives are threatened or the national security is at stake or some other equally compelling rationale. In both of the Middle East hostage-takings of recent years—at the Iranian embassy in 1979 and 1980, and the TWA plane at the Beruit airport in 1985—news organizations knew information that they did not publish or broadcast, sometimes after a request by the government and sometimes on their own initiative. Even so, the administrations of Jimmy Carter and Ronald Reagan criticized the coverage in both those cases, suggesting that journalists were making news rather than reporting it, practicing diplomacy, playing into the hands of the hostage-takers, and the like. Reporters and their bosses responded by arguing that they were responsible to their viewers and readers, not to the government, and that their jobs required them to judge what is the news.

The role of the press and the relationship between reporters and officials have changed as part of the change in the overall environment, not independent of it. Consider some of the relevant conditions:

(1) The organization of the news business has changed. Fewer conglomerates are controlling more outlets. There has been a substantial reduction in the number of daily newspapers, and more significantly a reduction in the number of cities with competing daily papers, from almost 90 of the latter in the 1950s to about 50 in the 1980s. Significant daily national mass media have emerged for the first time: *The New York Times, The Wall Street Journal,* the television networks, and, yes, *USA Today.* Television now competes with print as a major source of news. News is profitable. Management of the news therefore often comes from the worlds of marketing and sales, not journalism, and owners are often divorced from management. News organizations compete for advertising much more than for circulation or for editorial quality. The latter tend to be means to the end of profits where there is competition at all.

(2) Even the current Supreme Court has, on the whole, left unaltered a wide swath of protected First Amendment activity, insulating the press from accountability in areas such as libel and access.

(3) The United States is adjusting to a new role in the world arena. There is no longer U.S. or U.S./USSR hegemony throughout the globe. Protection of the national interest takes on a new meaning when the two superpowers are no longer running the show.

(4) The political parties have lost their primacy as the central organizing and communicating vehicles of American politics.

(5) Technology has made all kinds of communication possible instantaneously around the world. Hodding Carter tells a story that makes this point dramatically. As assistant secretary of state for public affairs during the Iranian hostage crisis, he recalls thinking about how the roles had reversed. Instead of reporters waiting outside his office to

get the news of what was happening abroad, he, the official spokes-
person for the government, was watching television along with millions
of others to find out what was going on.

(6) Journalism has become respectable. Today's reporters are often as
well-educated, upwardly mobile, and well-paid as the officials they
cover.

Of all these changes, two were identified in the Harvard study as
having been the most significant contributors to the change in the
press-government relationship. First, both officials and journalists
identified a change in the nature and attitude of reporters as particularly
important. The Watergate/Vietnam period represented what Albert
Hunt, a member of the advisory group for the study and the Washington
bureau chief for the *Wall Street Journal*, called a "sea change." He
measured the change along the same lines as did James Schlesinger, a
former secretary of defense: from an earlier, healthy skepticism, to a
more current, unhealthy cynicism on the part of the press. The argument
was that the performance of government in Vietnam and Watergate
contributed toward a cynicism on the part of the press that manifested
itself in the attitude and actions of reporters toward government. The
more cynical the reporters were, the more wary and secretive were the
policymakers. The more secretive the officials, the more aggressive and
cynical the reporters, and so on.

But if the attitude of reporters has changed the climate of the press-
government relationship over the last twenty years, the emergence of
television as a central medium of public affairs has had just as significant
an impact on the techniques and the routines of how reporters and
officials do their business with one another. Television has become so
much a presence that it it easy to forget how relatively recently it has
become a force in policymaking. It was only in 1962 that CBS and NBC
went to 30-minute nightly news programs. (ABC did not follow until
several years after that.) In those early years of the nightly network
news, what was in the morning newspapers would determine what
stories the networks would set out to cover for the evening program.
Now, programming innovations and technological advances have
changed that. Morning news programs on all three networks often make
news or advance stories, thereby providing the framework for the rest of
the media, including the newspapers, to pursue during the day.
Technological advances such as the use of tape, minicams, and live feeds
have enabled the networks to break stories and beat the newspapers to

the news, so that they are now doing their own share of agenda-setting for officials as well as for other journalists.

What is important to note about virtually all of the factors is that they have tended to push the press toward more influence and power in public affairs. Reporters may not have desired the current condition and may not even approve of it, but here it is. The institutionalized press has more to say about what happens in government than would have been imaginable fifty years ago. Officials today spend time with the press and think about press matters to a degree that would amaze their predecessors. Dealing with the press is simply part of their jobs.

One of the results of increased press power is that significant and specific impacts of the press can be demonstrated. We already noticed some specific impacts of the press in the Love Canal case. From our research, it has become apparent that some of the most significant impacts of the press occur early on the policymaking process, when it is not yet clear which issues will be addressed and what questions will be decided. Officials believe that the media do a lot to set the policy agenda and to influence how an issue is understood by policymakers, interest groups, and the public.

Policymakers also agree that the press affects the process of policymaking, although there is far less consensus among them about precisely how that impact is felt. The coverage of the media tends to have two specific impacts. First, the press speeds up the decision-making process. Second, coverage, particularly negative coverage, tends to push the decision making up the bureaucracy. Both of these impacts seemed to be at work in the Love Canal relocation decision.

However, policymakers do not say that the press has had an impact on their own policy choices. That is no surprise. Officials cannot be expected to identify instances when they altered their own best judgment because of influence they felt from newspapers and television.

To try to understand how the press affects policies themselves, we looked beyond the testimony of decision makers to see what happened in particular cases. We examined instances of policymaking where we thought the press played a role. In only three of the six cases that we studied in depth—the reorganization of the Post Office in 1969-1970, the decision of President Jimmy Carter to defer deployment and production of the neutron bomb in 1978, and the 1982 decision of the Reagan administration to reverse its own new policy in favor of tax exemptions for private schools that discriminate—did it appear that there was a significant impact of the press on the heart of the policy itself.

Even in these cases, the impact of the press tended to be on the likelihood of certain policy choices being adopted or implemented; thus the press appeared to affect the odds in favor of one option or another rather than being the dominant force in policy determination. From that perspective, and from the interviews with officials who gave us examples of where the press had influenced the policy choices of others, it appears that the press can have a substantial effect on the policy choice, as well as on the policymaking process.

The increased power and influence of the media in public affairs and the likelihood of specific press impacts entail important consequences for the press.

First, government officials will eventually internalize the same understanding and will spend more time learning how to deal more effectively with the media. Officials will learn that they have to be better at the communication aspects of their jobs in order to be better at their jobs. As a result, the press will have to become better at doing their jobs. Government officials more sophisticated in their press relations will pose new challenges for reporters in holding those officials accountable.

Second, for better or for worse, in a democracy new power carries with it new responsibility. This is not in the first instance external accountability, the responsibility to be answerable to government or to the public in new ways. It is what Max Weber called "the ethic of responsibility." Weber argued that in public life all ethically oriented conduct may be guided by one of two differing and irreconcilably opposed maxims: either toward an ethic of ultimate ends, where the means are irrelevant as long as the heart is pure and the goals are admirable; or toward an ethic of responsibility in which, in this case, journalists possess "a trained relentlessness in viewing the realities of life, and the ability to face such realities and to measure up to them inwardly."

Journalists themselves must begin to deal with this new power and new role. They must begin by acknowledging that they are not outside the process of governance and the business of public affairs. They must accept the consequent responsibility—not generally for the success of individual officials or policies, but more important, for the maintenance and preservation of the processes and institutions of government itself. This is their obligation as ethical professionals, whether or not they are happy about this new role.

Exercising that responsibility may change some of the conventions under which journalists now operate. For instance, I am reminded of an occasion when a respected senior editor at a major metropolitan daily newspaper was trying to explain and justify the coverage of the Middle East to a group of angry but decidedly civilized middle-class Jews. Someone in the audience complained about a particular story, saying that the article was fine but the headline was a terrible distortion. The editor agreed that the headline was off-base and acknowledged that headlines are very influential. "But," he responded, "do you know how late I would have to stay at the paper in order to write that headline?" The answer is unacceptable in an era of substantial press impact. The conventions of the business that permit a junior person to write the headlines and senior management to avoid responsibility for them while accepting their influence simply will not wash. It would not take much imagination to figure out how top editors could be responsible for the headlines without having to work 20-hour days or stay at the office until midnight.

Exit polls are another example. Political scientists, journalists, and politicians can argue forever about whether or not broadcasting early results affects turnout and voting decisions. That misses the point. What is crucial is that a lot of people believe that reporting those results before the polls close does have an impact. That perception in itself is enough. News organizations are familiar with criticism leveled at public officials because of the appearance of wrong-doing, even where there is no actual wrong-doing. Similarly, news organizations ought to understand that the appearance of undermining the electoral process is a problem in itself, whether or not it can be demonstrated to be the case.

Journalists ought to concentrate on new techniques of practicing their craft rather than expecting officials to cease managing the news. Officials have a responsibility to themselves and their programs to frame the issues and package information to serve those interests. Journalists often respond by charging that the officials are doing something evil and undemocratic, rather than by starting the harder task of rethinking their practices so as to be better able to deal with policymakers who are particularly adept at dealing with them. The complaints about Ronald Reagan are a case in point, and it is not surprising that the public has not been aroused by those complaints to urge the president to change his behavior.

The press might also think about eliminating anonymous sources, particularly those who deliver opinions and not facts, and collective commentators, as in, "Critics of the legislation say that . . . " Anonymous sources are used more for getting a good quote in a typical story than for protecting the unusual whistle-blowcr. Insisting on attribution may make life for difficult for reporters, but in the long run it will produce a more honest and responsive governmental system.

Editors might consider the fairness of the impact of stories on public attitudes toward government in their assignment and publishing decisions. Senator Paul Simon (D-IL) has pointed out that the typical insistence of the press on characterizing congressional foreign trips as unwarranted junkets has decreased the willingness of congressmen and women and senators to travel. As a result, the very people who should see first-hand situations in the rest of the world on which they have to vote are staying home. Staff and lame-duck members make the trips instead, if they are made at all. What about the impact on government itself? By regularly publishing internal memoranda disclosing the full range of policy options being considered, the press has forced policy-makers to put less in writing, to make decisions in a shorter time frame, and to include fewer people in the process. These results are not all or always bad, but they are the results. The media ought to consider whether the disruption is worth the publication. Good decision making requires some confidences and some secrecy that are not limited to the extreme cases where national security or human lives are at stake.

Perhaps the most overriding change in press conventions is in accepting the logical consequences of journalistic decisions. It is difficult for journalists to accept responsibility for what they do because it will encumber them in deciding what to publish, and they are probably right that some stories that ought to be published will be omitted. Yet here is an example of where accepting the consequences would have changed the story in an acceptable way.

A reporter for another major metropolitan daily newspaper recounted an instance where she and her newspaper agreed that they ought to publish the name and general address of a man who had been arrested for driving without a license because this was standard operating procedure at the paper in covering crime stories. But this was not just another crime story. The driver in question was a nonunion driver driving a bus during a bus strike that had become violent. The reporter said that she knew that publishing the information would put the man at risk, but that not to do so would require that the paper consider the consequences every time it published the name. So they went ahead, and the fellow suffered a horrible beating. The argument here is that following standard operating procedure in this case, as in the case of the non-headline writing editor, is unethical and unacceptable conduct. This is only tangentially a press and government story, but it makes the point.

At the very least, all of this means that journalists must satisfy us, all of us in government and out, that their decisions are being made in a thoughtful and reasoned process that takes into consideration the consequences of those decisions for the institutions and process of government and for the specific individuals and policies as well.

If the press does not accept this new reality, and does not change its ways of doing business in awareness of it, then I fear that this society will do what it has always done with institutions that are perceived to be too big for their britches and abusing their power: cut them down to size. The process is already beginning, with huge libel judgments, legislation in states and Congress restricting press access, and judges railing against reporters whenever the name of a rape complainant is broadcast, the secrecy of a grand jury is breached, or a juror is aggressively pursued by a reporter after a trial.

The responsibility is still right where it should be: with the men and women in the news business. The myths of distance and of adversariness ought finally to be put to rest. There can no longer be any illusions about whether or not the press plays a muscular role in policymaking, or whether we can identify specific and predictable impacts of the press. The only issue left is whether the press as individuals and as an institution can, in Weber's words, "face such reality" and act accordingly. Both the quality of the government and the nature of press freedom will be affected by whether they can rise to the occasion.

NOTES

1. A more comprehensive version of the story of the role of the press in the 1980 Love Canal relocation can be found in *How the Press Affects Federal Policy Making: Six Case Studies* by Martin Linsky, Jonathan Moore, Wendy O'Donnell, and David Whitman (New York: W. W. Norton, May 1986).

2. The analysis here is drawn from "Legislative Ethics and the Media: Historical Perspective," a paper presented to The Hastings Center Research Group on Legislative Ethics and the Media, June 2, 1983, at The Hastings Center, 360 Broadway, Hastings-on-Hudson, New York 10706.

3. For more on the history of objectivity in the press, see *Discovering the News* by Michael Schudson (New York: Basic Books, 1978).

4. The results of the project are presented in detail in *Impact: How the Press Affects Federal Policy Making* by Martin Linsky (New York: W. W. Norton, May 1986).

5. For example, in his brilliant biography of Walter Lippman, Ronald Steel reports on more than one occasion of Lippman being privately solicited for advice by those in power. For instance, Lippman recommended changes in John F. Kennedy's inauguration address and then wrote favorably about the speech after it was delivered (Ronald Steel, *Walter Lippman and the American Century*, Boston: Little, Brown, 1980, pp. 524-525). Kathleen Turner's recent book, *Lyndon Johnson's Dual War* (Chicago: University of Chicago Press, 1985), recounts in unsparing detail LBJ's efforts to woo the press, which included, sometimes unsuccessfully, soliciting their advice and awaiting favorable coverage that it was acceptable.

9

PRACTICING RESPONSIBLE JOURNALISM: COSMOPOLITAN VERSUS PROVINCIAL MODELS

Howard M. Ziff

On the evening of Wednesday, August 25, 1773, Samuel Johnson and his friend, James Boswell, arrived in Banff, on the North Sea coast of Scotland, en route to the Highlands and Western Isles. The Earl of Fife, who could be counted on to give the travelers "a very elegant reception," unfortunately was not at home. The friends were thus forced to spend the night in what Boswell (1961, p. 79) in his published account of the trip called "but an indifferent inn." Boswell's private journal, not published until the twentieth century, reveals that the principal complaint against the inn at Banff was that Dr. Johnson could not keep his windows open; he was, therefore, "constantly eager for fresh air."

The episode of the indifferent inn does not appear in Johnson's own published account of the trip, *A Journey to the Western Isles of Scotland*. However, in his account of Banff, Johnson (1775) veers off into a brief description of Scotch windows, particularly noting the difficulty of keeping them open. He comments that however elegant the homes of "our northern neighbours," a "stranger may be sometimes forgiven, if he allows himself to wish for fresher air."

Johnson (1775, pp. 44-45) then writes,

These diminutive observations seem to take away something from the dignity of writing, and therefore are never communicated but with hesitation, and a little fear of abasement and contempt. But it must be remembered, that life consists not of a series of illustrious actions or elegant enjoyments; the greater part of our time passes in compliance with necessities, in the performance of daily duties, in the removal of small inconveniencies, in the procurement of petty pleasures; and we are well or ill at ease, as the main stream of life glides on smoothly, or is ruffled by small obstacles and frequent interruption. The true state of every nation is the state of common life. The manners of a people are not to be found in the schools of learning, or the palaces of greatness, where the national character is obscured or obliterated by travel or instruction, by philosophy or vanity; nor is public happiness to be estimated by the assemblies of the gay, or the banquets of the rich. The great mass of nations is neither rich nor gay: they whose aggregate constitutes the people, are found in the streets, and the villages, in the shops and farms; and from them collectively considered, must the measure of general prosperity be taken. As they approach to delicacy a nation is refined, as their conveniences are multiplied, a nation, at least a commercial nation, must be denominated wealthy.

In addition to being a fine sample of Johnson's magisterial prose, this passage holds two particular points of interest for our purposes. First, it is infused with finely tuned, philosophic comprehension of the nature of a good report or account; the reporter has not only mastered what he is writing about but also why he is writing about it. In this case Johnson, professedly a strict adherent to the eighteenth-century notion that art is best that is most universal and abstract and with the widest possible moral applicability, explains why he includes a detailed account of something so particular as a Scotch window. The passage is also significant for the way it moves from apology for a form of prose accounting of the mundane to an apology, in the broadest sense, for the mundane itself: "The true state of every nation is the state of common life."

The following pages will examine two models of journalism, the *cosmopolitan* and the *provincial* , which, in some measure, parallel the contrast between the abstract "dignity of writing" and the particulars of Scotch windows that Johnson comprehended in his brief Banff essay. I hope particularly to hold the two models in balance, avoiding the danger of collapsing one into the other.

I

The immediate purpose of this essay is to answer a question: Should all journalists observe the same set of ethical standards and the same concept of social responsibility? That they do not is obvious. One has only to compare a school newspaper in Nepal, a government newspaper in Nairobi, and a general circulation newspaper in New York. These examples are drawn from diverse societies with diverse ends.

If we limit ourselves, however, to the established press, within our own national society, with all of its political, economic, and social constraints, should we not be able to enunciate universal principles, however vague, that can be the subject of fruitful study and debate and guide daily conduct, as the Hutchins Commission on a Free and Responsible Press was able to do four decades ago? Indeed, it has been the work of these past four decades to articulate just such universal professional standards of ethics and social responsibility, and an examination of the literature leads to the conclusion that, although certain local variations might be acknowledged, there is a consensus that uniformity in ethics and social responsibility ought to prevail.

An illustration of this consensus can be found in *Editors, Publishers and Newspaper Ethics*, a monograph written by Philip Meyer (1983). In it, Meyer surveys the role of news executives in making day-to-day ethical decisions in newspapers. It is his tacit assumption that all decisions are commensurable, that a universal context of choice prevails. For instance, Meyer notes that a very small percentage of newspapers, those with very large circulations, serve a very large percentage of all readers. Because he wanted to provide evidence of how ethical decision making has an impact in the aggregate on readers, he weighted his sample scientifically so that the larger the circulation of the newspaper, the more likely it would be that its executives would be surveyed. The tacit assumption in this procedure is that all editors and publishers are playing the same game and a distinction in size between newspapers is not relevant.

Within this consensus position, as I have suggested, there may remain the troubling question of local ground rules. Yes, all are playing the same game, but do local circumstances, such as the size of a journalistic enterprise, its economic autonomy, and the nature of the local community, call for local ground rules, local variations in the game?

How these local demands play themselves out is the subject of an essay, "Small-town Journalism Has Some Big Ethical Headaches" by Loren Ghiglione (1978), one of the more sensitive commentators on the press scene and himself a leading small-town editor-publisher.

Ghiglione finds small, community newspapers "more susceptible to certain kinds of ethical problems" than large, metropolitan newspapers, and throughout his discussion displays a sensitivity to local values and demands. Nonetheless, Ghiglione's essay, in logic and tone, is based on the assumption that a uniform set of professional standards ought to apply, uniform, at least, for a press in a democratic society.

I will argue that Meyer and Ghiglione are mistaken, that uniform professional standards of ethics and responsibility do not exist in fact and ought not exist in principle. I will argue, instead, that a diversity of journalism enriches a democratic society and that this diversity is exemplified not only by differences of political outlook and economic strength, but also by a wider diversity of ends, a variety of ultimate commitments and goals, which generate differing concepts of the ethical and responsible, and differing ways of imagining and accounting for community experiences.

Before I argue this point, however, I will examine in detail Ghiglione's point that smaller community newspapers are more susceptible to certain kinds of ethical problems and try to imagine how those problems might be resolved by the conventional notion of universal professional standards.

For some readers the following section may well provide an adequate account of ethical decision making in the face of local differences. For them, the argument is at an end.

II

DEALING WITH INDIVIDUALS

A range of ethical problems for both metropolitan and community journalists stems from their responsibility toward news sources and/or persons explicitly mentioned in the news. Invasion of privacy, observing confidentiality, and obtaining news under misleading or outright false pretences fall under this category. Each can be seen as a possible example of treating individuals not as self-determining subjects but as objects in the news. Specific examples include prurient prying into the sex life of a public or even a not-so-public figure, or obtaining private photographs by theft. Perhaps more typical are the daily, mundane examples of stories about which the sources or subjects (often the same persons) feel emotions ranging from annoyance to humiliated outrage, stories of traffic tickets, burglaries, suicides, bankruptcies, and so on.

What typically makes such stories more sensitive for smaller newspapers was summarized by an editor of a chain of small Connecticut weeklies: "They [big-city reporters] leave the bodies where they fall, we meet our victims face-to-face the next day in the local coffee shop."

Big-city journalists are more likely to have impersonal relationships with the individuals involved in the news. They live miles apart and often come together only because of what is about to become a news story: a robbery, white-collar crime, or fire.

To be sure, a big-city journalist, especially a beat reporter, might have daily contacts with the same persons, but these contacts are likely to be on what might be termed "grounds of professional interaction," a kind of mannered playing field in which each knows the rules. Within the wary limits of his or her professional skill and intelligence, the players are equals and conscious of the consequences of what they do or say.

This is less likely to be the case in a small town. The journalist there might buy groceries in the store that has been robbed, probably knows the family that had been burned out by a fire, and expects not only to interview a city councilor in his or her public role but also to run into him or her in the supermarket checkout line or at a PTA meeting, where both are in nonprofessional roles as parents.

"You have to maintain some distances as a journalist to be fair and objective," as one small-town reporter remarked, "but it's not the same distance you maintain when you live with people as neighbors day in and day out."

In discussing this problem, an adherent to the notion of journalism as a profession with a universal set of standards might argue as follows:

> Journalists should maintain a dispassionate professional distance in their relationships to news sources and persons who find themselves by happenstance subjects of the news. The disspassionate standard of the professional journalist, just as those of the doctor or lawyer, is in no way compromised if its limits are carefully defined, in the journalist's case to what is legitimately news, i.e., in the public interest. It must be acknowledged, however, that journalists, often are compelled to be the bearer of evil or embarrassing tidings and this can be a particularly acute problem in small-town settings. Just as a doctor or lawyer must tell a patient or client things they don't want to hear, so, too, must the journalist. This can be mitigated, however, not by less but by more professionalism. Journalists, for instance, can educate a news source such as a part-time town councilor, on the nature and consequences of their

mutual obligation. Indeed, they might even warn against and offer the opportunity to correct and refine an unguarded utterance. However, while professional standards leave ample room for avoiding unnecessary harm, the journalist's intelligent account of the day's event will inevitably include some bruised feelings.

FINANCIAL CONSTRAINTS

Smaller newspapers often plead economic expediency when they engage in practices that can give the appearance of compromising objectivity. A classic example is the junket, a trip to cover an actual or putative news event that is paid for not by the journalist's own news organization but by an interested party, such as a governmental agency, a food company, a sports team, a travel agency or tourist publicity bureau, or even a foreign government.

Other examples or practices that can give at least the appearance of compromising objectivity include the printing of public relations releases as a kind of "free news" that is virtually or completely unverified and unedited. A lenient policy permitting relatively poorly paid employees to accept gifts or a wide, possibly compromising range of outside, part-time employment are also characteristic of smaller rather than metropolitan newspapers.

Discussion of these practices usually includes a reference to the dilemma of smaller news organizations that may not have the resources to verify and edit "free news" or could not afford to pay for the kinds of opportunities that junkets provide for free. John Hulteng (1985) in *The Messenger's Motives* acknowledges for instance that "it is one thing . . . for the wealthy Los Angeles Times to assert . . . independence," but "smaller papers or local radio or TV stations face a tougher choice" (p. 41).

The example of junkets is typical of how standards are changing and becoming universalized. At one time in the not-so-distant past, news organizations rich and poor accepted them without qualm. Today, editor after editor rises to protest innocence of the practice, and the few remaining defenders (aside from the curmudgeons who insist that whatever the appearance, their motives are pure) usually do so by taking a pauper's oath. Even this moral means test is bowing to a relentless march of professionalism. Hulteng (1985, p. 41) notes, "An increasing number of publications and stations—in many cases prodded by their staffs—are making the hard decision on the side of ethics rather than expediency."

BOOSTERISM

All newspapers inevitably feel some pressure to support the home team, whether the team is literally a sports team or figuratively the local industry, the downtown shopping district, the local production of *The Mousetrap*, or a candidate for public office with local ties.

In the conventional view, the carrot for local boosterism is improvement in the culture and economy, and thus a potential increase in advertising and circulation base. The stick is a threat to withdraw advertising if the newspaper doesn't join in the cheerleading.

Large newspapers are popularly supposed to be less vulnerable to the pressures and temptations of boosterism. In part, this is because of their economic autonomy. They can afford to offend at least some individual advertisers, even groups of advertisers. Small newspapers, it is argued feel the pressure more immediately—it takes only a handful of advertisers, perhaps only one or two, to cause grievous economic injury. Similarly, editors and reporters on small newspapers are likely to meet the social pressure of boosterism in their daily interactions—the message of "let's all get behind the new park proposal" is delivered not only in letters to the editor and telephone calls and visits from dignitaries, but in the daily contacts in the lunchroom, grocery store, and filling station, and it is brought home from school by the kids.

It is not surprising therefore that although most of the literature of journalistic ethics and social responsibility condemns boosterism, there is a patronizing indulgence for the community editor under special local pressures. Those who support boosterism usually do so with a dodgy defensiveness that makes them easy targets of cosmopolitan satire.

COMMUNITY VALUES

The problem as to what extent, if any, it is part of ethical and responsible journalism to reflect the standards of the community in which a newspaper is published obviously takes different forms depending on just what those values and standards are.

When the *Boston Globe* supported integration of Boston's school system, it was out of step with the standards and values of a large portion, perhaps a majority, of the persons in the community of Boston. The debate was clear-cut and the values and standards of literally tens of thousands of Bostonians were volubly and sometimes violently made clear to the paper. (At one point in the conflict, a bullet was fired through a city room window.)

On the other hand, it is often the case that a large metropolitan newspaper is operating in areas in which there are few predominant community standards or values. The community is large and heterogenous. Among many choices, the newspaper may adopt the standards of the economic or the cultural elite, it may explicitly set itself up as an independent monitor of standards sailing by its own star, or may simply reflect the philosophy of an owner-publisher.

Further problems crop up when one considers that a due respect for community standards is a form of accountability to the community. Members of the staff of the community-based newspaper may not, for instance, be personally offended by printed obscenities or advertisements that show nearly nude persons. A large majority of the community may be. Is the newspaper surrendering professional standards and its own sense of responsibility by responding to the sensibilities of the community or is it being ethically accountable?

In many smaller communities the journalist's dilemma is still further complicated by the community expectancy that the journalists, just as any other good citizen, will involve themselves in community affairs. The editor of a large newspaper can maintain professional aloofness by refusing to serve on the board of the YMCA or volunteer to solicit funds for the local symphony in the sure knowledge that scores of other qualified persons are available to take his or her place. That editor can also count on the support of a large community of journalistic peers. Meanwhile, unexpressed beneficent impulses can be channeled into professional journalistic organizations and activities, and the defense of press freedom.

The editor of a small-town newspaper is not only more likely to be importuned to do community service, but he or she is also likely to feel a very personal pull toward such service. Their own children would be attending the arts classes of the local arts council; they are likely to want to work out in a new YMCA health facility; they may be intimately familiar, house by house, family by family, with the area for which a redevelopment grant is being sought. A principled refusal to serve the community is a bit harder to explain in such circumstances. Yet how can such services be rendered without compromising journalistic objectivity and independence of judgment?

There is no consensus on the proper approach to community service. Ghiglione, for instance, recounts his acceptance of a seat on a community board and ensuing problems. Most journalists who play an active role in the community activities do so on the explicit public understanding that it will not be allowed to compromise the independent judgment of their news organization.

III

In the previous section, I examined ethical dilemmas to which smaller news organizations appear to be more susceptible than larger ones. I also might have elaborated the difference through a catalog of contrasting problems that are more likely to occur in metropolitan settings—the excesses brought about by competition, complex issues involving national security, and the like.

I have further tried to present what I think is the consensus view of those journalists who may acknowledge local differences, but who insist on thinking of journalism as a profession that is or ought to be governed by universal standards of ethics and responsibility.

It is likely that many readers, although questioning the adequacy of the discussion thus far, nonetheless agree that this cosmopolitan model suggests the proper way to deal with ethical problems, including those to which a small community newspaper or news organization is susceptible, namely, as journalistic professionals adhering to general professional standards.

A few, however, may still feel uneasy, may have a sense that our analysis is simply not morally satisfying. Somehow the texture of the problems seems to have been inadequately described; the standards applied do not quite fit morally and aesthetically with the experience of the journalists in the community as they know it.

It was argued, for instance, that certain stories that give pain to innocent individuals must nonetheless be published if they represent "what is legitimate news"; yet some may still feel compelled to open that forbidden Pandora's box and ask, "But what is news?"

I intend to keep the box resolutely closed, but not, I hope to ignore the basic ethical problem. Is not the source of our discomfort simply that we do not think of journalism as an autonomous profession, with professional standards and ethics and uniform goals? Instead, journalism may be thought of as a body of technique that serves diverse ends, one of the most common of which is provincialism.

The word "provincialism" is perhaps ill chosen, rounded as it is with pejorative connotations of narrowness and limited perspective and imagination. This aspect of provincialism, as Josiah Royce (1969) has pointed out in an unjustly neglected essay by the same name, is closely allied to the problem of self-centered individualism in any form of activity. Obviously, the province and individual must be aware of their duty to the whole, but to discharge that duty best they must also be loyal to themselves.

Royce (1969, p. 1084) writes,

> Philanthropy that is not founded upon a personal loyalty of the individual to his own family and to his own personal duties is notoriously an abstraction. We love the world better when we cherish our own friends the more faithfully. We do not grow in grace by forgetting individual duties on behalf of more remote social enterprises. Precisely, so, the province will not serve the nation by forgetting itself, but by emphasizing its own duty to the nation and therefore its right to attain and cultivate its own unique wisdom.

It is with Royce's healthy definition of provincialism in mind that provincialism itself, the maintenance, correction, and adornment of the local community and reverence to the sources of one's cultural being, can be offered as an end of journalism. The distinction is what lies behind a remark of an Upstate New York editor who, in discussing a rival newspaper in a nearby county seat, remarked, "We are part of the world of journalism, they are just part of the community."

Remove that "just" and you have two loyalties, two life choices of equal moral validity, neither of which is inherently better than the other, both of which have their unique sets of problems and possible pitfalls.

To be sure, journalists operating in either model have ethical and social responsibilities in common, responsibilities that, however, are not unique to journalism. It is important to have this clearly in focus, the difference between responsibilities that all journalists in our society should meet universally because they are the responsibilities of all citizens—journalists, electricians, and pensioners alike—and those responsibilities that are particular to the journalist and the ends he or she chooses to pursue.

For instance, the American Society of Newspaper Editors in its Statement of Principles says "Every effort must be made to assure that the news content is accurate," and calls for prompt and prominent correction of errors in fact and significant omissions. Similarly, there is a consensus among journalists against duplicitous dealing with news sources such as lies, disguises, theft of papers and photographs, and the honoring of pledges of confidentiality. Journalists are also called upon to deal ethically with their audiences, including using good taste and avoiding indecency. None of this reasonably implies a specific professional journalistic body of ethics, for none of the principles just enunciated is peculiar to journalism. Accuracy and making amends for inaccuracies is part of the obligation all of us—not just journalists— ought to feel toward our fellows. We all ought to avoid duplicitous dealings. Honoring promises, avoiding indecency and conduct that is gratuitously offensive to the taste of others—these, too, are ethical obligations of all persons.

To be sure, some of these obligations or the failure to meet them might have particularly weighty consequences for journalists. For instance, if my neighbor is casual and inaccurate in telling me over the back fence what he heard last night during the president's televised address, his transgression is not as significant as that of a newspaper that might make the same error. A risque joke has a different standing when told in the living room among consenting adults than when appearing on the pages of a newspaper.

There are also prudential, professional rationales for observing universal ethical standards. Telling the truth and keeping promises are believed to add to a newspaper's credibility, and the argument runs, "If we lose our credibility we may lose part of our audience and thus sales and profits."

Yet, however we weigh the importance of adhering to these ethical principles for newspapers, we still must acknowledge that the principles themselves do not flow from "the world of journalism" but have deeper roots and wider applicability.

When we turn, however, to principles and responsibilities that are more specific to the vocation of journalism, we find that those that apply to the cosmopolitan, professional model do not necessarily apply to the provincial model. In the first instance we are concerned with responsibilities and ethical considerations that can act as moral regulators of the autonomy upon which we insist for journalism as a profession, and not surprisingly we come up with principles such as objectivity and disinterestedness. In the latter, we set as as our goal service to the community and province, and will often find that our moral obligation is to be subjective and compassionate.

The ethical problems to which smaller newspapers are susceptible, that we have discussed above, we now find have been cast in terms of loyalty to the first model. When we think in terms of the provincial model, some disappear altogether.

Boosterism would still be condemned, of course, if it involved falsehood or suppression and misrepresentation of fact, evils that should be avoided for nonjournalistic as well as journalistic reasons. But much that would be condemned under the professional, cosmopolitan model would simply pose no problem to the provincial model. As Royce (1969) pointed out, "boasting is often harmless and may prove a stimulus to good work."

He continues:

> It is therefore to be indulged in as a tribute to our human weakness. But
> the better aspect of our provincial consciousness is always its longing for
> the improvement of the community. (p. 1085)

Similarly, the "problem" of community service by members of a news organization devoted to the second model is dissolved not simply as a tedious abstraction but as a plain irrelevancy. The organization is by its very nature devoted to community service, and its executives and employees would naturally be expected to participate on a wider basis if they are so inclined.

If a news organization is primarily devoted to community service, moreover, it would have no need to apply a moral means test before accepting at least some junkets. The sports writer might innocently travel to the out-of-town high school football game on the team bus as a nonpaying guest if she found it convenient; the agricultural writer might readily accept a state-sponsored trip to a university experiment station.

On the other hand, some junkets, perhaps most, would remain beyond the pale; for instance, those that work exclusively to serve the profit of persons or organizations who want to draw resources from the community, for example, a travel agency trip to New York; or those used to influence community opinion on matters about which the local news organization does not intend detailed, localized judgments, for example, a Defense Department weapons briefing.

The provincial news organization would also not need to justify use of certain kinds of public relations releases simply on grounds of economic necessity. It may well decide with Samuel Johnson, that the most vital interests of its audience lie in the compliance with necessities, the performance of daily duties, the procurement of petty pleasures, and the removal of small inconveniences, including the garbage. It might even recognize an obligation to further the therapeutic practice of well-informed gossip—and thus fill a daily page with club news, community service announcements, marriage announcements, birth notices, school menus, and the like, all gathered from local organizations and residents.

The provincial newspaper, moreover, should also have a concrete agenda for improvement of its community—better teaching in local schools, blocking a super highway bypass it considers unnecessary and destructive of a neighborhood, attracting new industries, a medical clinic, more business to the downtown shopping district. News coverage that explicitly forwards that agenda flows naturally, responsibly, and ethically from the concern for the community good.

It is doubtless true that a "longing for the improvement of the community," as well as less noble motives, too often leads to the suppression of facts. The provincial newspaper should not engage in these practices for prudential reasons. Even if they might have demonstrable short-term advantages, if discovered they are likely to hinder rather than advance the cause that supposedly justified them. More important, the reasons are based on its own ethos of community good—because suppression, misrepresentation, and failing to give voice to the inarticulate create further mistrust, and defeat the precious goal of sustaining the sense of community upon which all community interests are justified.

The problems of how a news organization treats individuals in the gathering and publication of news, promise keeping, confidentiality, and treatment of potentially embarrassing events are just as acute for a provincial newspaper as for a cosmopolitan professional one, but the context and fabric of sensibility differ with the news organizations' differing ends.

The standards of judgment on the surface may resemble that of a conventional cosmopolitan newspaper; however, local differences and sensibilities are not ad hoc exceptions, but woven into the very activity.

Thus such issues as when to name crime and suicide victims and how to treat details of sex crimes when a public official's private life has become a source of legitimate public interest are decided on the basis of local standards and traditions, and a sensitive avoidance of inflicting unnecessary pain is guided not by abstractions but by experience of the community itself.

It is, however, the problem of a news organization and its relation to the deepest community values that takes the most interesting form if we conceive of provincial journalism as having different ends from cosmopolitan professional journalism. This is because in a theoretically pure form, the professional model exists regardless of community values and the provincial exists because of them.

The cosmopolitan professional insists on an objective and dispassionate accounting of the news, and may stand above local values in its editorials to give the praise or condemnation that appears due from the autonomous viewpoint of "the world of journalism." The provincial newspaper, however, is implicated in local values and if it feels it must criticize a deeply held community value, it does so for the benefit of other, deeply lived communal beliefs. Thus the local southern editors who courageously opposed racism, such as Ralph McGill, did so not to destroy the way of life of their communities but to preserve and improve what they considered best in those communities.

At one level the problem for both cosmopolitan and provincial journalists as to when and under what circumstances they must place themselves and their organizations in opposition to a dominant local value or tradition involves a narrow prudential concern about when keeping the goodwill of the audience must give way to the call of conscience. For the provincial journalist, however, the problem can take on even more poignancy when conscience calls for changes so sweeping as to destroy the essence of the very community to which they have committed themselves. They might stand and fight and suffer the fate of an Elijah Lovejoy, the abolitionist editor who was murdered in 1837 by a proslavery mob, or they might suffer a typical twentieth-century fate— involuntary or, perhaps more tragic, voluntary exile. The tragedy of exile is particularly poignant because so many who suffer it can never free themselves, indeed do not want to free themselves, from a deep longing for the culture that bred them and to which their voice and being are so firmly attached. Such had been the fate of literally thousands of journalists in our own time. Exile is also a fate shared by many of the great literary artists of modern times, including Joyce, Mann, Milosz, and Singer.

The history of American journalism is replete with examples of self-imposed exile, men and women who felt compelled to shake off their provincial backgrounds, who sought wider, cosmopolitan opportunities. Yet, how often it is the Niles, Michigan, of a Ring Lardner, the California of a Lincoln Steffens, the Hannibal of a Mark Twain that are the ironic reference points of their cosmopolitan successes.

It is a great sadness of American journalism today that however diverse their geographic background and polished their skills, so many journalists are valued because they are interchangeable; they put themselves behind the word processor in whatever city to which they are called by corporate employers. The unique value of each person and each region is thus endangered by a system of replaceable parts, and we are in danger of losing sight of the simple truth that the fact that you cannot move a Mike Royko from Chicago or a Jimmy Breslin from New York is a sign of their towering strengths as journalists.

IV

The greatness of provincial journalism is in its capacity to reflect "the true state of every nation . . . the state of common life." This is most obvious in small newspapers that are literally published in the provinces, but it is also true of large newspapers and news organizations that are unabashedly committed to a community or a community of interest. Such news organizations may well think of themselves as cosmopolitan, but their ethics and social responsibility over time serve narrower and deeper "provincial" audiences. One thinks of the *Wall Street Journal*, *Variety*, or the *Christian Science Monitor*, each of which serves an international community, but in terms of a "provincial" community of interest. One thinks also of sophisticated and provincial organizations such as the *Louisville Courier Journal*, the *Des Moines Register* and *Tribune*, and the *Boston Globe*, each of which has won cosmopolitan professional honors, but each of which has as its primary ethos, responsibility to, and no small measure of affection for, its own province.

Great journalistic organizations and moral journalists are not necessarily engaged in the same endeavour, traveling toward the same specific goal. One thing they share in common, however, is loyalty toward their vision of how the fabric of experience can best be explicated, what stories it is necessary to tell ourselves to realize the ideal significance of our communal life. Because success, moral success, must always be measured by effort and intention as well as achievement, lest we despair, the moral journalist ought also to share Samuel Johnson's tacit insistence upon self-awareness, a striving to understand exactly what it is we are doing—why we think news is news—and his attachment of ideal endeavor to the mundane stuff of everyday life.

REFERENCES

Boswell, J. (1961). *Boswell's journal of a tour to the Hebrides with Samuel Johnson, L.L.D. 1773* (F.A. Pottle and C.H. Bennett, Eds.). New York: McGraw-Hill.
Ghiglione, L. (1978). Smalltown journalism has some big ethical headaches. In B. Rubin (Ed.), *Questioning media ethics*. New York: Praeger.
Hulteng, J. (1985). *The messenger's motives* (2nd Ed.). Englewood Cliffs, NJ: Prentice-Hall.
Johnson, S. (1775). *A journey to the western islands of Scotland*. London: W. Strahan.
Meyer, P. (1983). *Editors, publishers and newspaper ethics*. Washington, DC: American Society of Newspaper Editors.
Royce, J. (1969). Provincialism. In J. J. McDermott (Ed.), *Basic writings of Josiah Royce, Volume 2*. Chicago: University of Chicago Press.

SELECTED BIBLIOGRAPHY

Questions concerning mass media responsibility lead the scholar to theories from a number of different fields. Selections from applied and professional ethics, ethical theory, political and social philosophy, and representation theory are included here.

Parts of Sections I and II have been distributed by The Hastings Center, Institute of Society, Ethics and the Life Sciences at the Working on Teaching Journalism Ethics, held in Rye, New York, in June 1984, at the AEJMC/Gannett/UK Workshop on Teaching Journalism Ethics, July 1984. Parts will be published by the Silha Center on Media Ethics and Law, University of Minnesota. Clifford Christians in the primary author of these sections. Everette Dennis is the sole author of Section III.

SECTION I
APPLIED AND PROFESSIONAL ETHICS

Bayles, M. (1981). *Professional ethics*. Belmont, CA: Wadsworth.

> General overview of the ethical issues that concern professions in general: obligations to clients and the public, relationships between professional norms and classical ethical principles, duties to maintaining a profession's vitality, the nature of service, regulation, discipline of unprofessional behavior.

Callahan, D., & Bok, S. (Eds.). (1980). *Ethics teaching in higher education*. New York: Plenum Press.

> This is the first of the Hastings Center Series in Ethics, and consists of the background papers of The Hastings Center Project on the Teaching of Ethics. It contains an account of the history of ethics teaching; general issues and problems in current curricula; and specific topics such as teaching undergraduates, professional ethics, paternalism, and whistleblowing.

Goldman, A. (1980). *The moral foundations of professional ethics*. Totowa, NJ: Rowmand & Littlefield.

Goldman's question is whether professional ethics are of a unique kind. In developing such an ethics, do we construct special norms and principles or work within the givens of general moral theory? Professionals themselves tend to assume a strong differentiation, but Goldman argues for continuity. He elaborates his thesis with separate chapters on medical, legal, business, and government ethics.

Jarvis, P. (1983). *Professional education*. London: Croom Helm.

Jarvis examines the wide range of skills, knowledge, and attitudes that are necessary components of professional education. He discusses the need for preprofessional studies to embrace a professional ideology without indoctrination.

Regan, T., & Van Deveer, D. (1982). *And justice for all: New introductory essays in ethics and public policy*. Totowa, NJ: Rowman & Littlefield.

This volume addresses a broad range of theoretical and practical issues. Essays on "Utilitarianism" and "Individual Rights" outline general moral principles; chapters on "Homosexuality," "Nuclear Power," "Reverse Descrimination," and others describe specific policy questions. The final chapters explore the nature of a just society and the concept of "the rights of man."

Stanley, M. (1981). *The technological conscience: Survival and dignity in an age of expertise*. Chicago: University of Chicago Press. (pub. orig. 1978)

A contemporary classic in focus on education as a tool for liberation from the technocism that dominates our culture. Indebted to Heidegger, Stanley insists on human dignity as a pretheoretical given. He makes useful distinctions between social and cultural dimensions, and provides worthwhile interpretations of Paulo Freire.

SECTION II
ETHICAL THEORY
POLITICAL AND SOCIAL PHILOSOPHY

NOTE: Works of classical philosophers are listed with no annotation.

Ackerman, B. (1980). *Social justice in the liberal state*. New Haven, CT: Yale University Press.

Ackerman attempts to provide systematic philosophical foundations for the liberal state. Rejecting social contract theory and utilitarianism, he relies on the notion of a dialogue between persons making competing claims on scarce resources. His main emphasis is on distributive justice, but he also discusses genetic engineering, abortion, population control, and affirmative action.

Aristotle. *Nicomachean Ethics.*

Baier, K. (1967). *The moral point of view: A rational basis of ethics.* New York: Random House.

Baier explains moralities as forms of practical reasoning and social control. He provides procedures for making ethical decisions that include examining reasons, abstracting rules of reason, and using those rules in a prima facie sense in making personal and social decisions.

Bok, S. (1979). *Lying: Moral choice in public and private life.* New York: Vintage.

Bok examines the many types of situations where deception becomes an issue. She provides a justificatory method by which a person can test potentially deceptive practices and argues for the need for general honesty.

Bok, S. (1982). *Secrets: On the ethics of concealment and revelation.* New York: Pantheon.

Here, the author examines the notion of secrecy as it pervades personal and public life. She explores questions of when confidentiality should be maintained and when it should be breached. The book includes an excellent chapter on the risks of investigative journalism.

Bowie, N. (Ed.). (1985). *Making ethical decisions.* New York: McGraw-Hill.

This anthology includes an excellent selection of excerpts from classical ethical works and articles from current moral philosophers. The book provides an easy introduction to ethical theory. Bowie's introductions to each section help the novice understand the basic questions and factors that reflect in personal ethical dilemmas.

Callahan, D., & Engelhardt, H. T., Jr. (Eds.). (1981). *The roots of ethics, science, religion and values.* New York: Plenum.

The essays in this book are taken from the earlier four-volume series published by the Hastings Center on "The Foundations of Ethics and Its Relationship to Science." The series included the following: I. *Science, Ethics and Medicine*; II. *Knowledge, Value and Belief*; III. *Morals, Science and Sociality*; IV. *Knowing and Valuing: The Search for Common Roots.*

Caplan, A., & Callahan, D. (Eds.). (1981). *Ethics in hard times.* New York: Plenum.

This volume in the Hastings Center Series in Ethics addresses questions on the scope, content, and purpose of ethical inquiry; the role of the state vis-à-vis the citizen; and the morality of policy issues in a pluralistic society.

Childress, J. (1982). *Moral responsibility in conflicts.* Baton Rouge: Louisiana State University Press.

Childress examines the different reasons that are offered to override some duties or responsibilities and support others. He uses three instances of conflict—nonviolence, war, and conscientious objection—to illustrate the various moral justifications claimed to legitimize certain viewpoints.

Dewey, J. *Human nature and conduct.*

Feinberg, J. (1980). *Rights, justice, and the bounds of liberty.* Princeton, NJ: Princeton University Press.

This collection of previously published essays and papers by Feinberg covers issues in social and legal philosophy, bioethics, rights-theory, and the theory of justice. The author analyzes the nature and value of rights; the relationship of rights to freedoms, duties, and obligations; rights-claims and the rights of animals; the right to be born and the right to die; and the relationships between liberty, paternalism, and various formulations of "harm."

Fishkin, J. (1982). *The limits of obligation.* New Haven, CT: Yale University Press.

Fishkin contends that the basic structure of individual morality and responsibility is incompatible with general obligations to society. In situations where large numbers of people are involved we need to rethink what actions—from minimum altruism to heroic sacrifice—are appropriate.

Fisk, M. (1980). *Ethics and society: A Marxist interpretation of value.* New York: New York University Press.

An ambitious attempt to develop a Marxist ethics with a neutral rather than technical vocabulary on which broad agreement can be based. He argues that priority must be given to fulfilling people's essential needs. Primarily interested in elaborating the grounds for a relativistic ethics in which self-interest is served. Its theoretical scope and completeness rivals that of Rawls's *Theory of Justice.*

Fried, Charles. (1981). *Contract as promise: A theory of contractual obligation.* Cambridge, MA: Harvard University Press.

Fried specifically considers the notion of contract within a legal context, but the theoretical foundations he presents for that context are applicable in many more informal situations, including implicit promises made by government and by the institutional media.

Goodpaster, K. E., & Sayre, K. M. (1979). *Ethics and problems of the 21st century.* Notre Dame: University of Notre Dame Press.

These original essays address the problems associated with applying ethical theory to social and environmental issues.

Jonas, H. (1984). *The imperative of responsibility: In search of an ethics for the technological age.* Chicago: University of Chicago Press.

Currently the most debated book on ethics in Germany. Jonas believes that technological developments (nuclear weapons and international information) demand a new ethics that takes seriously our imminent destruction and global solidarity. He grounds our responsibility in a purposive nature that we are morally bound to preserve. This is a compelling argument that must be confronted by those in media who make freedom the paramount good.

Kant, I. *Fundamental principles of the metaphysics of morals.*

Kohlberg, L. (1981). *Essays on moral development, Volume I: The philosophy of moral development.* San Francisco: Harper & Row.

Subtitled "Moral Stages and the Idea of Justice," Volume I of this proposed series elaborates on Kohlberg's theory of moral development. His thesis is that the moral idea of justice can be wholly embodied and accounted for within the six stages of moral development from his theory. He examines the relativity of value judgment, the role of education in moral development, and the application of moral principles to political, legal, philosophical, and religious problems.

Kupperman, J. (1983). *The foundations of morality.* London: George Allen & Unwin.

This is a compelling rationale for ethical theorizing. While common sense morality is not based on a clearly articulated theoretical foundation, morality cannot be critiqued or improved without redesigning the foundations. The book is primarily an attempt to explain the nature of ethical knowledge and articulate the ways in which ethical claims can be challenged and justified.

Lyons, D. (Ed.). (1979). *Rights.* Belmont, CA: Wadsworth.

The anthology contains essays by current philosophers on the nature of rights. The essays examine the nature of rights, claims for natural and self-evident rights, rights and justice, and the enforcement of rights.

MacIntyre, A. (1981). *After virtue: A study in moral theory.* Notre Dame: University of Notre Dame Press.

This is a provocative book that has been the best-selling volume in philosophy in recent years. MacIntyre's thesis is that Enlightenment individualism continues to dominate modern Western culture, and individual autonomy precludes the development of substantive ethics. Exceptional scholarship on Aristotle and persuasive regarding Marx.

Mill, J. S. *On liberty.*

Moltmann, J. (1984). *On human dignity: Political theology and ethics* (Trans., M. Meeks). Philadelphia: Fortress.

Moltmann is a major contemporary theologian who has been a foremost proponent of human rights. Important attempt to wrest human rights from its highly politicized context and establish it, instead, in a notion of human dignity. Emphasis on basic human needs, freedom, and community. He is particularly concerned about the relationship of freedom and power and includes an important chapter on meaningful work.

Nozick, R. (1974). *Anarchy, state, and utopia.* New York: Basic Books.

Nozick presents a powerful defense of the "minimal state," arguing that the violation of individual rights brought about by the interference of the state can rarely be justified. He proposes a new theory of distributive justice and an integration of ethics, legal philosophy, and economic theory into a unified political philosophy.

Olshewsky, T. (1985). *Foundations of moral decisions: A dialogue.* Belmont, CA: Wadsworth.

This little book introduces the novice to ethical inquiry through an annotated dialogue format. Although the issues are within the realm of medical ethics and the dialogue participants are a physician, a lawyer, and a chaplain, the fundamental ethical theories raised are applicable to other situations. The annotations and study questions provide excellent introductory access to classical philosophy. The dialogue illustrates how the classical principles are reflected in discussion of practical issues.

Plato. *Gorgias.*

Rawls, J. (1971). *A theory of justice.* Cambridge, MA: Harvard University Press.

The major twentieth-century theory of justice, offering an alternative to the utilitarian conception. The principles of justice Rawls sets forth are those that, he claims, the reasonable person would choose, were he cloaked in a "veil of ignorance," unaware of his own social status and natural assets and liabilities.

Simmons, J. A. (1979). *Moral principles and political obligations.* Princeton, NJ: Princeton University Press.

Simmons reviews major theories in political and moral philosophy, from Locke through Nozick, examining the problem of political obligation. He finds that principles of consent, fair play, gratitude, and the duty of justice cannot justify claims that most citizens have obligations of duties to support and comply with our political institutions. He argues that questions of political obligation may be resolved only after appeals to moral considerations other than political obligations.

Sullivan, W. (1982). *Reconstructing public philosophy.* Berkeley: University of California Press.

This volume documents clearly the crisis at present in individual liberalism. Sullivan takes issue with such leading representatives of philosophic liberalism as Robert Nozick, John Rawls, and Lawrence Kohlberg. His point is to formulate an alternative. He labels that option "civic republicanism" and demonstrates how civility, justice, dignity, and self-government are still latent in the democratic landscape.

Taylor, P. W. (1975). *Principles of ethics: An introduction.* Encino, CA: Dickenson.

Well-written chapters for beginners. Provides helpful definitions of ethics, morals, and values. Good overview of utilitarianism and Kantian ethics.

Williams, G. L. (Ed.). (1976). *John Stuart Mill on politics and society*. New York: International Publications Service.

SECTION III
MEDIA ETHICS

Alley, R. S. (1977). *Television: Ethics for hire?* Nashville: Abingdon.

Based on interviews with Norman Lear, Alan Alda, Earl Hammer, and other prominent television producers. Provides insight into the aims and ethics of industry pacesetters in areas such as violence, pornography, and materialism.

Callahan, D., Green, W., Jennings, B., & Linsky, M. (1985). *Congress and the media: The ethical connection*. New York: The Hastings Center.

Casebier, A., & Casebier, J. (Eds.). (1978). *Social responsibilities of the mass media*. Washington, DC: University Press of America.

Proceedings of a conference on mass media responsibility sponsored by the University of Southern California. Two or three general chapters on professional rights and obligations. The others deal with specific issues in journalism (presidential elections, coverage of women and ethnic groups) and entertainment programming (pro and antisocial images, controversial content, responsibility of producers).

Christians, C., & Covert, C. (1980). *Teaching ethics in journalism education*. New York: Hastings Center Monograph.

Surveys the state-of-the-art in ethics teaching and reviews substantive issues in journalism ethics today. Outlines four instructional objectives.

Christians, C., & Gjelsten, G. (1981). *Media ethics and the church*. Kristiansand, Norway: International Mass Media Institute.

Proceedings of an international conference represented especially by Third World countries. Includes theory, print media, broadcasting, advertising, performing arts, and the International Information Order.

Christians, C., Rotzoll, K. B., & Fackler, M. (1983). *Media ethics: Cases and moral reasoning*. New York: Longman.

A total of 76 case studies and commentaries are presented on the major ethical issues in news, advertising, and entertainment. Includes an introductory chapter on "Ethical Foundations and Perspectives." The Potter Box is used as a device for reaching ethically justifiable conclusions.

Communication (1981). Volume 6.

This special issue of the journal contains a variety of articles on media ethics both in the United States and abroad.

Elliott, D. (1984). *Toward the development of a model for journalism ethics instruction.*
Ann Arbor, MI: University Microfilms International.

Provides a detailed description of three methods for teaching journalism ethics.
Elliott proposes a trifoundational theory based on moral obligations to society,
peers, and to oneself. Includes an assessment of the literature in journalism ethics.

Gerald, J. (1983). *News of crime: Courts and press in conflict.* Westport, CT: Greenwood.

The author examines the institutional behavior of the mass media and the courts in
criminal cases, looking primarily at the conflict between news of crime and the ideal
of the fair trial.

Gerald, J. (1963). *The social responsibility of the press.* Minneapolis: University of
Minnesota Press.

Views mass media as a social institution and attempts to evaluate how effectively
they are serving society. The proposals for improvement that arise from his review
are substantive and complex.

Goldstein, T. (1985). *The news at any cost: How journalists compromise their ethics to
shape the news.* New York: Simon & Schuster.

A journalist's account of press misbehavior. Goldstein uses a number of case
studies to raise questions about journalistic behavior in such areas as ambush
interviews, conflict of interest, fabrication, and plagiarism.

Goodwin, H. E. (1983). *Groping for ethics in journalism.* Ames: Iowa State University
Press.

Explores a variety of issues such as conflicts of interest, deception and misrepresentation, privacy and incompetence. Based on interviews with a wide-ranging sample
of professionals and academics, and a review of the codes and literature. Calls for a
set of principles that can guide the journalism profession.

Haselden, K. (1968). *Morality and the mass media.* Nashville: Broadman.

Attempts to apply an enlightened Christian moral perspective to mass media
contents, dealing especially with censorship, sex, obscenity, commercialism, and
violence.

Heine, W. (1975). *Journalism ethics: A case book.* London, Canada: University of
Western Ontario Library.

Twelve case studies gathered largely from the British and Ontario Press Councils.
They cover such topics as advertising, invasion of privacy, secret documents,
sensational photos, and the reporting of scandal. Official responses and legal
opinions are included for a few cases.

Hulteng, J. L. (1981). *Playing it straight: A practical discussion of the ethical principles of
ASNE.* Chester, CT: Globe Pequot Press.

The author examines the Statement of Principles of the American Society of
Newspaper Editors through a discussion of cases. The principles include freedom
of the press, responsibility, impartiality, and fair play.

Hulteng, J. L. (1985). *The messenger's motives: Ethical problems of the news media* (2nd Ed.). Englewood Cliffs, NJ: Prentice-Hall.

Surveys the standards by which today's media operate, and investigates how successfully they live up to these guidelines distilled from contemporary codes and accepted practices. Looks at the ethical problems of those who write, edit, produce, and report in print and broadcasting.

Journal of Mass Media Ethics.

New journal initially published twice yearly; available from Ralph Barney, Department of Communication, Brigham Young University.

Lambeth, E. (1986). *Committed journalism: An ethic for the profession.* Bloomington: Indiana University Press. (advance copy not available for annotation)

McCulloch, F. (Ed.). (1984). *Drawing the line.* Washington, DC: American Society of Newspaper Editors.

A joint project of the Poynter Institute for Media Studies and the American Society of Newspaper Editors. The book contains 31 case studies written by editors who describe their most difficult ethical dilemmas.

Merrill, J. C. (1974). *The imperative of freedom: A philosophy of journalistic autonomy.* New York: Hastings House.

A provocative exploration of the philosophical roots of journalistic ethics in which the author's dedication to libertarian ideals comes through strongly.

Merrill, J. C., & Barney, R. (Eds.). (1975). *Ethics and the press: Readings in mass media morality.* New York: Hastings House.

A collection of articles and addresses concerned with ethical considerations in reporting news. Part One deals with philosophical and theoretical issues; Part Two presents ethical dilemmas faced in everyday journalism.

Merrill, J. C., & Odell, S. J. (1983). *Philosophy and journalism.* New York: Longman.

Eight chapters in which substantive issues regarding the journalism profession are treated philosophically: logic, semantics, epistemology, morality, axiology, rhetoric, political theory, and metaphysics.

Meyer, P. (1983). *Editors, publishers and newspaper ethics.* Washington, DC: American Society of Newspaper Editors.

Report of comprehensive research into publishers' attitudes toward ethics as compared with those of editors. Discusses four types of publishers—politician, partisan, statesman, absentee—and investigates their values regarding selected ethical issues and case studies. Includes a generous amount of the data in the final section.

National Ethics Committee, Society of Professional Journalists, Sigma Delta Chi. *Journalism Ethics Report.* Chicago: Society of Professional Journalists.

Published annually since 1981, this report includes both original articles and reprints on the subject of journalism ethics activities throughout the nation.

Phelan, J. M. (1980). *Disenchantment: Meaning and morality in the media.* New York: Hastings House.

Phelan proposes that a public philosophy ought to arise from the humanities that can address issues of new media technology and cultural freedom. He contends that media ethics ought not to be reduced to codes and to professional dilemmas, while neglecting theoretical foundations.

Rivers, W. L., Schramm, W., & Christians, C. G. (1980). *Responsibility in mass communication* (3rd Ed.). New York: Harper & Row.

A classic text on media ethics first published in 1957. Argues for social responsibility theory, which means freedom from government and from business constraints in order to serve society through the principles of fairness and truth. Includes a case study on minorities and makes recommendations for the government, media, and public.

Rubin, B. (Ed.). (1978). *Questioning media ethics.* New York: Praeger.

Collection of general articles on journalism ethics, plus coverage of specific problems such as the fairness doctrine, stereotyping of women, the Third World, and small-town journalism. Two comprehensive chapters describe the ways journalists have been portrayed in motion pictures.

Schmuhl, R. (Ed.). (1984). *The responsibilities of journalists.* Notre Dame: University of Notre Dame Press.

Papers and speeches presented at a Notre Dame Conference. Mixture of media professionals, journalism educators, and ethicists. Schmuhl introduces the volume with an essay on the history and nature of responsibility.

Shaw, D. (1984). *Press watch.* New York: Macmillan.

This book contains essays written by the media critic and published in the *Los Angeles Times.* The author reflects on various ethical dilemmas for the media including confidentiality, deception, prizes, and court coverage.

Swain, B. M. (1978). *Reporters' ethics.* Ames: Iowa State University Press.

Readable summary of the ethical problems faced by 67 reporters from 16 metropolitan dailies who were interviewed by the author.

Thayer, L. (Ed.). (1973). *Communication: Ethical and moral issues.* New York: Gordon and Breach.

A compilation of addresses given at the University of Iowa in 1969-1970 by well-known academicians. Concludes with an attempt to sketch out the direction an "Ethics of Communication" should take theoretically.

Thayer, L. (Ed.). (1980). *Ethics, morality and the media.* New York: Hastings House.

Twenty-seven essays and speeches—mostly by practioners—on the current status of media ethics. Includes a long introduction by the editor, "Notes on American Culture." Covers film, newspapers, magazines, radio, television, and advertising.

SECTION IV
REPRESENTATION THEORY

Birch, A. H. (1971). *Representation*. New York: Praeger. Bibliography, footnotes, index.

Disputing Pitkin's view that the various types of representation can be synthesized into one basic form, Birch stresses their distinctiveness. He proposes a framework consisting of four types of representation and eight functions that representation serves. (Types: symbolic, delegated, microcosmic and elective; Functions: responsiveness, accountability, peaceful change, leadership, responsibility, legitimation, consent, relief of pressure.) This framework, says the author, will assist in value-free empirical research.

Commission on the Freedom of the Press. (1947). *A free and responsible press*. Chicago: University of Chicago Press.

Stresses accountability of the press to the citizenry. "The need of the citizen for adequate and uncontaminated mental food is such that he is under a duty to get it. . . . [The press] must be accountable to society for meeting the public need and for maintaining the rights of citizens and the almost forgotten rights of speakers who have no press" (pp. 17-18).

"An over-all social responsibility for the quality of press service to the citizen cannot be escaped; the community cannot wholly delegate to any other agency the ultimate responsibility for a function in which its own existence as a free society may be at stake" (p. 126).

Says press is obliged to give a representative picture of the various groups that make up society.

Dennis, E. E. (1980). The rhetoric and reality of representation: A legal basis for press freedom and minority rights. In B. Rubin, (Ed.), *Small voices and great trumpets: Minorities and the media*. New York: Praeger. Footnotes.

Considers minority criticism of the press in order to ask whether the press should accurately represent the society and its component parts (1) in terms of the representativeness of news content, (2) in terms of newsroom personnel, and (3) in terms of the press as a representative of the public.

Distinguishes between the mass media of general dissemination and the specialized press, then argues for a constitutionally based mandate for the press to provide a full picture to the minority communities. Press freedom is a personal constitutional right that cannot be enjoyed by most people unless there is a full and responsive press to channel information.

Dennis, E. E. (1974, Spring). The press and the public interest: A definitional dilemma. *De Paul Law Review*, XXIII, 937-960. Footnotes.

Surveys definitions of public interest, especially that of Virginia Held, and asks whether public interest and the interest of the press are one and the same. Traces the emergence of a public interest doctrine in American law that gives the press relief from damages in such areas as libel. Finally, proposes a model for reconciling the two.

Dennis, E. E., & Ismach, A. (1981). Representational realities. In *Reporting processes and practices* (Chap. 13, pp. 304-307). Belmont, CA: Wadsworth.

Reporters both represent and are representative of public, but reporters are clearly not a cross-section of the community. Discusses the problem of the disparity between what readers say they view as important and what they actually read.

Hocking, W. E. (1947). *Freedom of the press: A framework of principle*. A report from the Commission of the Freedom of the Press. Chicago: Chicago University Press.

The author, a member of the Commission on the Freedom of the Press (see separate entry above), argues that there are no rights without responsibilities. Speaks of "the moral right of a people to be well served by its press" and "a right of the public to be served with a substantial and honest basis of fact for its judgments of public affairs" (pp. 168-169).

Quotes Supreme Court opinions relating to press responsibility. Describes Soviet conceptions of the role of the press.

Pitkin, H. F. (Ed.). (1969). *Representation*. New York: Atherton.

Pitkin's introduction surveys views of representation held by various political theorists, including Hobbes, Rousseau, Simon Sterne, M. C. Swabey, H. F. Gosnell, Rene de Visme Williamson, A. P. Griffiths, E. Burke, and J. S. Mill, all of whose works are excerpted in this selection (see separate entries by author).

Pitkin also discusses various metaphors for representation: mirror, map, painting, symbol.

Pitkin, H. F. (1967). *The concept of representation*. Berkeley: University of California Press. Bibliography, footnotes, index.

Does not discuss the media specifically, but acknowledges that "institutions and practices which embody some kind of representation are necessary in any large and articulated society, and need have nothing to do with popular self-government." Concentrates on political theories of representation, including those of Hobbes, Edmund Burke, and Liberalism. Defines the term as "the making present *in some sense* of something which is nevertheless *not* present literally in fact."

Discusses conflicting notions of the relation between representative and constituents: Should the former be free to act as he or she pleases (Hobbes), should he or she make decisions for (that is, instead of) his or her constituents, or should he or she reflect accurately the wishes and opinions of those he represents?

Rivers, W. L., Peterson, T., & Jenson, J. W. (1971). *The mass media and modern society* (2nd Ed.). San Francisco: Rinehart. Bibliography, index.

A historical survey of views of the press; also chapters on media and government, media as informers and interpreters, and media as persuaders.

Siebert, F. S., Peterson, T., & Schramm, W. (1956). *Four theories of the press.* Urbana: University of Illinois Press.

> In essays written separately, the authors describe four theories of the press. In "Authoritarian," the oldest of the four, truth is conceived not as the product of the great mass of people, but of a few wise people; the press functions from the top down, as a servant of the state. (Siebert)

> In "Libertarian," the right to truth is an inalienable right; the press is conceived of as a partner in the search for truth, a presenter of evidence and arguments on the basis of which people can check on government. (Siebert)

> In "Social Responsibility," a descendant of the Libertarian view, the power and near monopoly position of the media impose on them an obligation to be socially responsible. If not, it may be necessary for some agency to enforce it. (Peterson)

> In "Communist," the press is the state-owned tool of the ruling power. (Schramm)

Tuchman, G. (1978). *Making news: A study in the construction of reality.* New York: Free Press.

INDEX

ABOUT THE CONTRIBUTORS

Ralph D. Barney, Chair of the Department of Communications at Brigham Young University, was born and raised in Arizona. He has journalism degrees from Brigham Young University (B.S.), University of Iowa (M.A.), and the University of Missouri (Ph.D.). He has worked in newspapering (Salt Lake City and Honolulu) and in public relations and advertising (Hawaii). A number of papers have been published on both international communication and ethics topics. He coedited with John C. Merrill *Ethics and The Press* (1976) and is coeditor, with John J. Black of Utah State University, of the new *Journal of Mass Media Ethics*. He has served as a Fulbright Scholar at the University of South Pacific in Suva, Fiji, in 1981, teaching basic communication courses, and has been Fellow at the East-West Communication Institute in Hawaii on two occasions.

Clifford G. Christians is an Associate Professor of Communications at the University of Illinois—Urbana. His research interests are professional ethics, philosophy of technology, popular culture, and humanities approaches to communication research. He has authored *Media Ethics: Cases and Moral Reasoning* (with Kim Rotzoll and Mark Fackler), *Responsibility in Mass Communication* (with William Rivers and Wilbur Schramm), and edited *Jacques Ellul: Interpretive Essays* (with Jay Van Hook).

Everette E. Dennis is Executive Director of the Gannett Center for Media Studies at Columbia University. Formerly he was Dean of the School of Journalism at the University of Oregon, and Professor of Journalism and Mass Communication at the University of Minnesota, where he had a joint appointment in American Studies. Author or coauthor of 11 books and more than 60 journal articles, Dennis was a Liberal Arts Fellow at the Harvard Law School and held two other Harvard postdoctoral appointments.

Deni Elliott is on faculty in the Department of Communication at Utah State University. Her academic degrees include a B.A. in Communication from the University of Maryland, a master's degree in Philosophy and graduate work in education at Wayne State University, and a doctoral degree in Philosophy of Education from Harvard University. She has experience in journalism, public relations, and advertising. She has conducted seminars on ethics for editors and reporters, student journalists and journalism educators. Her writings on ethics have appeared in trade, academic, and scholastic publications.

Theodore L. Glasser is on the faculty of the School of Journalism and Mass Communication at the University of Minnesota, where he also serves as Associate Director of the Silha Center for the Study of Media Ethics and Law. His articles have appeared in a variety of academic and professional publications, including *Journalism Quarterly, Journal of Broadcasting, Communications and the Law, Policy Sciences, The Quill,* and *Nieman Reports.* He is currently Chair of the Mass Communication Division of the International Communication Association and a member of the Accrediting Council on Education in Journalism and Mass Communication. He received his Ph.D. in mass communication from the University of Iowa. He has been on the Minnesota faculty since 1981.

Louis W. Hodges is Professor of Religion and Director of a program for preprofessional students, "Society and the Professions: Studies in Applied Ethics," at Washington and Lee University. He received his Ph.D. in religious studies from Duke University in 1960. Since 1974, he has taught full-time in the applied ethics of business, journalism, law, and medicine. He is editor of an annual publication on applied ethics entitled, *Social Responsibility: Business, Journalism, Law, and Medicine.*

Martin Linsky is Lecturer in Public Policy at the John F. Kennedy School of Government, where he teaches courses on the media, legislatures, and public management. He is Faculty Chairman of the school's training program for senior executives in Massachusetts government, and Codirector of a project at the school that is creating a management training and development plan for the Commonwealth of Puerto Rico. He has just completed a three-year research project on how the press affects federal policymaking, the results of which are forthcoming in *Impact: How the Press Affects Federal Policy Making,* and *How the Press Affects Federal Policy Making: Six Case Studies.*

His former positions include Executive Editor of *The Advocates*, Public Broadcasting's show; Assistant Director of the Institute of Politics at Harvard; Editor of *The Real Paper* in Cambridge; and Editorial Writer for *The Boston Globe*. In addition, he has served as Member and Assistant Minority Floor Leader of the Massachusetts House of Representatives and Assistant Attorney General for the Commonwealth of Massachusetts. His publications include *Television and the Presidential Elections*. He is a graduate of Williams College and Harvard Law School.

John C. Merrill is Professor of Journalism and Philosophy at Louisiana State University. He has taught journalism, English, and philosophy in five universities for some 35 years, the longest period at the University of Missouri. He is the author or editor of fifteen books and several hundred journal articles, many of them in the areas of ethics and international communication. His Ph.D. (mass communication) is from the University of Iowa.

Howard M. Ziff is Director of Journalistic Studies at the University of Massachusetts—Amherst. He has also taught at the University of Illinois—Urbana and the Graduate School of Journalism of Columbia University. His journalistic career includes reporting and editing for *The Chicago Daily News* from 1958 to 1968. His articles and columns have also appeared in *The Washington Post, New York Times,* and *Boston Globe*. He has authored several articles and was an editor of *Evaluating the Press,* winner of a Sigma Delta Chi, Society of Professional Journalists award for excellence in research.